The Return of the Ashes

The Return of the Ashes

MIKE BREARLEY, O.B.E.
& DUDLEY DOUST

PELHAM BOOKS
London

To Horace and Midge Brearley
and
Jane Doust

First published in Great Britain by
Pelham Books Ltd
52 Bedford Square
London W.C.1
1978

ISBN 0 7207 1066 9

Filmset and printed in Great Britain by
BAS Printers Limited, Over Wallop, Hampshire

Contents

Acknowledgements

The authors would like to thank Norman Harris, Ted Braun, John Hughes, and especially Hugo Young, for their help and advice during the preparation of this book

Illustrations

All the photographs in this book are by Patrick Eagar, except those on page 17, those of Richard Scholar on page 25, and those otherwise credited

Foreword

Dudley Doust

The main problem in a first-person narrative is that without using other people's insights and opinions, not to mention a shaving mirror, the first person rarely sees himself as others see him. Modesty forbids. Memory distorts. Perhaps it will be helpful then, to stand back, and draw a rough verbal portrait of the Middlesex and England captain, before the reader begins Mike Brearley's own account of the return of the Ashes.

First, the shaving mirror. The face he sees in the mirror is friendly, sensitive, intelligent – and a little doleful due to its length. His eyes are hazel, his thick black hair is prematurely flecked with grey. The first hint of resolution is gathered in his strong jaw. He uses an electric toothbrush which he found useless, for years, until he realized it was powered by batteries.

Brearley habitually cranks his long neck and often flings a scarf round it in the way of an undergraduate. When he speaks, sometimes only after long deliberation, his voice is soft and his remarks often are qualified with a veritable thesaurus of adjectives, as though he has been turning over pebbles, searching for the clearest, most unflawed, most precise and, above all, best balanced opinion to plop into a pool of conversation. His accent might perhaps be described as 'middle-classless', appropriately, because he looks on himself as his own man, neither Establishment nor anti-Establishment: an uncomfortable position in 1977.

In what will doubtless be one day seen as a landmark season in the history of cricket, Brearley took the role as a mediator among players, the established authorities, the disruptive promoter Packer, new English patrons to the game and the Press. Altogether, it was a thankless burden for a new captain to take on as well as setting out to win the Ashes.

Brearley is sometimes thought to be fair to a fault. If he writes an autobiography, its title should be *On the Other Hand*. I spoke once to one of his favourite dons at Cambridge, the philosopher John Wisdom. Wisdom spoke of Brearley with respect and affection and then concluded of his former scholar-sportsman:

'Brearley was a fair-minded and sympathetic man. He never set out to demolish another man's argument and, before making any objections, he would look for something valuable in what the man was saying. I should think he also applies this in cricket.'

A city-boy, Brearley on the other hand, and with usual fairness, loves the countryside – although he is chary of dogs and touches a pony's nose with only two fingers. In the view of my young daughters, he is a 'nice man and not at all big-headed'. They once struck a bargain with him. If he did the washing-up, they would saddle-soap the new walking boots he was taking on holiday to the Himalayas. They struck a poor bargain; he would have done the dishes anyway. He brings a bottle of wine when he comes to visit, remembers your daughter's birthday with a card and returns from India with a lacquered wooden box for your wife.

Does all this make a good cricket captain? It helps. Clearly the brain-power helps, too, and the generous persuasion of his personality. A captain at School, University, and of a touring Under-25 MCC side, Brearley had largely abandoned cricket, in order to teach philosophy at the University of Newcastle (where he began his Ph.D. thesis on 'Emotion and Reason': a conflict central to sport).

Suddenly, in 1971, he returned to full-time cricket as captain of Middlesex: a philosophy don come in to smooth the ruffles between younger and older members of the side. New players came, others left or retired and somewhere along the way players no longer were wearing coats and ties. In this informal atmosphere, Middlesex won the county title in 1976, and shared it in 1977. 'He's a good Test captain,' says one of his England colleagues, 'because he went through a baptism of fire at Middlesex.'

So, too, did he go through a baptism of fire leading England in 1977. The team obviously responded to Brearley. Cricketers may not talk freely with an outsider but surely they don't band together before giving a stock answer to a stock question: Why was he successful? 'Mike,' said each, 'gets the best out of his players.' One added, 'Mike never belittles you. He makes you feel you're the man for the job.' A most telling observation came from a man who has played under many England captains: 'Brearley doesn't flap,' he said. 'He always seems in control, on and off the field. That's a rare quality among captains.'

Why is a non-cricket writer collaborating on the book? The idea of such a project grew out of an article I wrote on Brearley in *The Sunday Times* when, over an interview that extended through a showery day at Lord's on through dinner, we found common ground in our interest not only in sport but also in its role in life. We also discussed different techniques of sports-writing, some of which are employed in this book.

Finally, there are a few comments to be made on the structure of the book. We wrote some sections individually, some together, some with the help of recollections of other players on the England side. The italicized paragraphs that precede some chapters are scene-setters, outside the mainstream of the first-person narrative. Mike Brearley has made all the photographic selections, and commented on each: a rare thing, I think, in a sports book.

Ston Easton
Somerset

1 The Ball that Won the Ashes

'And here's Hendrick again. Running in to bowl to Marsh. 63 not out. Marsh swings, high on the off side. Randall's underneath it. This could be the Ashes for England. He's caught it! They've won. Randall turns a cartwheel. The stumps are seized by the players. The crowd comes onto the field and England have regained the Ashes.'

Christopher Martin-Jenkins, 15 August 1977, to millions of listeners to BBC Radio 3, the BBC World Service, and the Australian Broadcasting Company.

England have drawn the First Test, won the next two and now, as the pavilion clock at Headingley approaches 4.40 on the fourth afternoon of the Fourth Test, they have 85 runs and an innings in hand. Australia are hanging on: 248 for nine wickets. England captain Mike Brearley, hands behind his back, shifts from one foot to the other at first slip.

All day, or at least since we got Greg Chappell out, I had felt certain we would

'It all went haywire'. Puzzle: where's Bob Woolmer off to?

Left to right: Underwood (clutching the ball), Marsh (congratulating me), me (with stump), Woolmer, Knott (with bails), Boycott (guarding his cap) and Ealham (12th man). The other men with sticks are going to put a rope round the square

win, but the question was 'when?'. We had just got past an awkward stretch when Max Walker and Rodney Marsh were scoring all too freely. We became ragged; a catch was dropped; it was a frustrating situation. Now Marsh was still there, and could slog along for another 40 or 50 and, conceivably, put us in tomorrow for a paltry target. We would be sharper, I remember thinking, if they needed 50 to win with three wickets standing. I felt tired. I had stayed up late the previous night with Kerry Packer. I also felt a sense of anticlimax. The series was ending, not with a bang, but a whimper.

Marsh, perhaps a trifle resigned but pugnacious all the same, hunched over the crease. He would be taking the fifth ball of the over from Mike Hendrick, with Len Pascoe, a poor batsman, at the non-striker's end. Marsh was left with a choice: either nudge the ball for a single and retain the batting at the other end, and thus face Willis, or try to score fours. We were not worried about boundaries at this stage of the match, yet the man must be got out. Marsh hits the ball so hard that even when it goes in the air, you need a bit of luck for it to find a fielder. I briefly considered my field-placing. Were they set deep enough? Do I bring them in to cut off the single or push them back for the big hit? I had Derek Underwood and Derek Randall at mid-off and straight extra-cover, orthodox enough to pacify Hendrick but still deeper than usual.

The ball was lobbed back to Hendrick.

What about short square-leg? When Marsh plays defensively he pushes forward with his bat a bit low and close to his pad. It might go bat–pad to short square-leg. A quick snatch of the ball and the Ashes would be won. Woolmer was there, waiting. Woolmer is unique. He is the only bat–pad fieldsman I know who will take up a position *exactly* four yards from the batsman. The first time he does so in an innings, he will pace it out, make his mark and stand there until Doomsday and never complain. Woolmer is a brave fielder.

Hendrick began his stride towards the football-stand end, reflexly shining the ball down the groin of his flannels. The second new ball was only one over old and, for all that shining, its lacquer would show no useful wear on one side before a few more overs. It was comforting to know that, should we need it, the ball would retain its fire well after tea-time.

Hendrick is a big, gangling man with a big stride, and in the past he has been plagued with hamstring and groin injuries. Perhaps these breakdowns went a way towards explaining a view he expressed on bowling. 'Mike,' he had asked a fortnight earlier, on being selected for the Third Test, 'could you limit my spells to six or seven overs?' And now here he was, striding back towards his mark, fresh as a daisy, although earlier he had bowled ten overs in about 1 hour and 20 minutes, his longest spell of the series. Now I had had to bring him back sooner than I had hoped.

My admiration for Hendrick had grown innings by innings through the series but that afternoon I had learned something surprising about him. I had suggested he bowl an over of in-swingers at Robinson. 'When I let the ball go,'

Hendrick replied, 'I'm not sure which way it's going to move, in or out.' I was amazed that this was true of the finest fast-medium bowler in England.

Hendrick had now reached his mark. He turned and paused. He drew breath and set himself. He told me later what went through his mind at the moment: Marsh is having a slog at almost anything and if I bowl it anywhere near straight he will slog it into the air or miss it altogether. He said to himself: 'decent line, decent length, off-stump.'

Beside me, Alan Knott dangled down into position, feet together, gloves low, head up in that singular way of his. Woolmer went into his crouch, remarkably low, his eyes fixed on the roll of the front pad of the batsman. Tony Greig crouched. My hands were clammy. I wiped them down my flannels and crouched.

Hendrick came in. I remember thinking, as I often do as he thunders towards us: 'Hendo, your stride looks too long to be comfortable'. He lifted himself to his full height, and bowled what he later said was a 'crap' ball. Knott, with his usual precision, recalls it as just short of a good length and headed 18 inches outside the off stump. Woolmer, seeing Marsh swing, instinctively covered up, elbows up, eyes clamped shut. Marsh got a top edge and skied the ball. He let loose a foul, Aussie oath.

That was it. As Hendrick said, everything went haywire. I watched Randall take two strides to get under the ball. Out of the corner of my eye I could see Underwood sprinting, possibly half-skipping, towards him to congratulate him on the catch. As for the catch, I'm not certain I saw Randall take it. I had an eye on the stumps. Earlier in the over I had asked Knott to save me one but, in the turmoil, I made certain of the souvenir myself by pulling it out of the ground.

Randall said later he thought he might finish the match, capture the Ashes with flair, by leaning forward to take the catch behind his back. He thought better of the idea. Photographs depict him grabbing the ball like grim death just above the breastbone. Then he did something that reflected his anxiety at the moment. He kept his grip on the ball a split-second too long so that when he threw it, or meant to throw it, high and ceremoniously into the air, it went over his shoulder. Randall then turned his cartwheel which, doubtless, will remain a prevailing image of the Ashes of 1977. I wish I had seen it. It is something I had been coaxing him to do at some opportune moment throughout the series. He had been afraid of both the selectors' and the public's opinion but now, at the most opportune time, he had done it.

Underwood, in the meantime, grabbed the ball and jammed it into his pocket. He recalls little else of the moment. To this day, for instance, he cannot remember whether he picked the ball clean out of the air or caught it up on the bounce. More surprisingly, for weeks he believed it was Willis, not Hendrick, who bowled the last ball. I think this reflects *his* special state of torment at the time. He had been unsettled throughout the match by a running joke, to the effect that if the Packer players, Greig, Knott and himself, hoped to be picked for the final match at the Oval, England must intentionally lose at Headingley. Only in that way could the Ashes be kept in the balance.

Meanwhile, back at the crease, Knott was unperturbed at the moment of triumph. He plucked the bails off the stumps, one at a time, and, he says, stood guard over the two remaining stumps for the umpires to collect. At the other end, I'm told, Hendrick gathered up a wheatsheaf of stumps. Souvenirs were being reaped. The photographer Patrick Eagar later wondered why we hadn't designated at lunchtime who would get which souvenir; after all, there were eleven players and eleven possible momentoes: six stumps, four bails and a ball. The answer is that we never thought of it. Perhaps we couldn't plan beyond winning the match, perhaps such a scheme would have courted disaster.

In the mêlée, with spectators running onto the field and players running towards the pavilion, it crossed my mind that my stump could be used as a weapon. A weapon against what, I later thought: the oncoming crowd, the cameras and Pressmen, the scheduled meeting that evening with Packer and David Evans? The conflicts of the summer were not ending, after all, with the return of the Ashes.

The dressing-room was briefly a quiet haven. Away from the mob, the sense of victory sank in. A table was laid out with bottles of champagne. A cork popped. Willis – I'm sure it was Willis, he's always popping corks – raised the foaming bottle into the air and poured a toast all round. I went into the Australians' dressing-room and said something vapid, something like, 'Bad luck, lads. And thank you very much.' The Australians were gracious, but dismal all the same, sitting there on the benches, legs stretched out after eight weeks of battle, exhausted, watching on television what was happening only a few feet away. They drank cans of beer.

I don't much like visiting opponents' dressing-rooms after a match; if you have lost you feel uneasy, if you have won you feel worse. I withdrew to our own which had by now come very much to life. Willis, whose nickname is 'Goose', flapped round the room like a manic bird. He would stop to shake somebody's hand, fold his thumb into his palm and then, when it was taken, apologize: 'excuse the wart.'

It was a time for silly emotional release. I took Hendrick's hand and solemnly told him Peter West of the BBC awaited me on the balcony. What should I say to the nation? Hendo had perfected a jabberwocky language through the summer and he replied, deadpan, 'Say it was a heavy day. Say the strawson was good and there was a certain amount of swing in the spur-da-baldin.'

On the balcony, as elsewhere, Greg Chappell was the model loser. He said something appropriate. Whatever it was, I am not certain I caught it all. We could hardly hear each other, or Peter West, for all the chanting that rose from beneath us. 'Boycott! Boycott! Boycott!' It might have been opening night at Covent Garden. He made his balcony call in his vest. 'Boycott! Boycott! Boycott!'

Greg Chappell and the
author, interviewed
straight after the
Headingley game.
Photograph by
Ken Kelly

Inside, Chris Old stood at the edge of the celebration. He felt an intruder since he had missed the last two Tests with a shoulder injury. He had not come to join in the party but to congratulate *us*. I've always liked Chris, he's the warmest and most generous of men. We pulled him out onto the balcony for a cheer from the Yorkshire crowd. We all made our balcony calls. Randall flexed his muscles for the cameras. Willis poured champagne over my head and squirted it down on the crowd.

Knott, who sometimes celebrates with brandy and lemonade, allowed himself a ration of champagne and then, back inside, he gave one of his souvenir bails to Ian Botham who had come off earlier that afternoon with a fractured toe. Botham, only 21 and the youngest player in the side, hobbled up with his foot in a plastic bag of ice.

Headingley celebrations. Left to right: Underwood, Randall, Brearley, Hendrick, Willis, Woolmer (mainly obscured), Roope, Greig, Botham, Knott

He apologized for not telling me early in the match that his foot was under medical treatment and I said I understood his eagerness to play but that a captain should be informed of such things. Botham looked sheepish. Greg Chappell came in at that moment to give Ian a stump. It was from the Third Test at Trent Bridge, a reminder of the match in which Botham had taken five wickets in his first Test appearance.

Twelve brace of grouse, which Ian's father-in-law had cleaned over the weekend, lay in polythene sacks in the corner. On the past Saturday, the Glorious Twelfth, a chauffeur had appeared at the pavilion with the grouse and a blood-stained note. The note read as follows:

'Dear Mr Brearley,
My friends and I would like you to have some of these grouse and we'd like to congratulate you on your performance.

Sincerely,
(signed) Devonshire.'

The Duke of Devonshire, apart from being President of Derbyshire County Cricket Club, obviously was a good shot as well. His grouse were getting high. They still had to be distributed among the players. So, too, was the £9,000 gift arranged by the company director, David Evans.

Knott, easily the most composed of the Packer players, sat in his corner, sorting out socks. Give Knotty a thousand identical white socks and, without fail, he will find his own pair. At the moment, it was amazing how serenely he was going about this everyday task. Underwood was subdued. He switched from champagne to beer. Greig was upset. He said Alec Bedser had just asked him if he was available for the forthcoming tour of Pakistan and New Zealand. He took it as an ultimatum: either you break away from Packer, or you won't be picked for the Oval. Was it true?

Suddenly I realized that now, after the Ashes were won, some people felt we should break up the England team because of the Packer Affair, or have new players tried out for the forthcoming tour of Pakistan and New Zealand. I was angry. I was angry because at this very moment of celebration, newspapermen began to fire the question at me: 'who would play at the Oval?'. How did I know? I was only one of five selectors. I think I made my feeling plain that the team that won the Ashes should stick together for the final Test match. In my mind, I vowed to pursue my point, if necessary, among the other selectors.

We returned to the balcony one more time and standing there, gazing down over the sea of faces, I felt as though I was seeing it all from a great distance. There was something strange about the occasion. It was like moments remembered from the past: players running for the stumps, people swarming onto the field, and great crowds beneath the pavilion balcony. The heroes of my childhood had won the Ashes and been exalted, and now we had done the same thing.

I think it was Underwood who left the pavilion first. He wanted to get down the motorway and home to play in a county match for Kent. With him went the last ball which he planned to engrave and mount. It stands in his living room which commands a lovely view of the green hills of Kent. I have my stump. It is in my London flat. One day I may have it hinged and hung on the wall but, in the excitement, I forgot to have it autographed by the members of each team.

Headingley crowd, below pavilion. Ashes come home!

2 'If You Go on Like This . . .'

I cannot tell you the moment Compton struck his blow, off Morris, towards the boundary to win the Ashes at the Oval in 1953. Almost certainly I was with my family on holiday in Bognor Regis but this historic cricketing moment of my youth was swallowed up, long ago, in a confusion of photographs, films and stories. What I do recall vividly of the series is the heroic stand put up by Watson and Bailey, 196 runs through much of the last day, to achieve a drawn Second Test at Lord's. I recall it by its association. On 30 June 1953 I sat much of the afternoon listening to a radio broadcast of the match in the waiting room of the ear, nose and throat department of Charing Cross Hospital. I was eleven years old and in a few weeks' time I was to undergo a sinus operation.

Lord's is my home ground now and, in a manner of speaking, it was then because my father, Horace Brearley, played two first-class matches four years earlier for Middlesex. Actually, he is a Yorkshireman, born in Heckmondwike, near Dewsbury, the eighth of eight children. His father, in turn, must have been an able cricketer. A story is told of my father once getting a century in a Yorkshire league match. Someone came up to him afterwards and said, 'Well played, lad. But tha' wouldn't have got a hundred if tha' father had been bowling.'

Along with reading maths at the University of Leeds my father played for years in the Yorkshire second eleven. He finally played one first-class match for the County. It is recorded in the Wisden of the day. Yorkshire v Middlesex, July 1937, match drawn; Brearley, batting at number 5, scoring 8 and 9 runs. What later impressed me was the company he kept those days: Sutcliffe and Hutton for Yorkshire, Edrich and Compton for Middlesex. In all, seven past or future Test players appeared in that match.

My mother, Midge Goldsmith, was a Surrey girl. She read maths and played netball at London University. I was born on 28 April 1942 in Harrow, Middlesex. Almost immediately we moved to Portsmouth where my father was stationed in the Navy. After the war we returned to London where, at the age of about four, I experienced what now is my earliest vivid memory. In our house in Ealing there was a big wooden table under which one would take shelter in the event of an air raid. 'If a bomb falls on the table,' I remember asking my mother, 'will it save me?'

In 1950 my father became maths master and master in charge of cricket at the City of London school. He played club cricket at Brentham. A good all-round sportsman, I suspect he was a keener competitor than he now might like to think. I can remember him more than once letting me take a 20–16 lead in table

'Randall clutched it to his breastbone'

Above: Willis' barrage against Chappell, who looks nicely in control here. Perfectly balanced hook-shot

Left:

Bob Willis. Not a technically superb action, rather open-chested. He is looking inside his left arm. His action is very quick, and as a result it is not easy as a batsman to pick up the line of the ball early. Bob moves the ball in to the batsman if it swings, and occasionally it goes away off the pitch. He makes excellent use of his height

Right:

Chris Old. Excellent follow-through, hand low, fingers still straight, head steady and looking at the batsman. A good study in concentration

Jeff Thomson. Fine picture just before delivery. The ball, partly visible behind his left heel, is obscured from the batsman until very late in the delivery, so that, as with Willis (but for quite different reasons), it is not easy for the batsman to pick up the ball. Some very fast bowlers, notably Holding and Lillee, have such smooth and orthodox actions that the batsman does get an earlier and uninterrupted view of the ball. Notice the catapult-like effect of the long back-swing, and the high left foot to create maximum leverage. Jeff is beautifully sideways-on, head steady, looking round his left arm with that mean look at the batsman

tennis and then, buckling down, beating me 22–20.

I used to play any ball game that came my way but for a long while I was obsessed with cricket and football. 'If you go on like this,' my mother said when I was about 11, 'you'll end up doing nothing but playing cricket and football.'

I came from a very secure, conventional, friendly and warm family composed of my parents, two younger sisters and myself. But there were constraints placed on extremes of emotion. For example, when I was about 12 I was watching Billy Graham on television and becoming moved by his utter conviction of his ultimate place in Heaven. I hoped my father wouldn't come into the room. I was afraid he would tease me for watching such apocalyptic poppycock. I grew up embarrassed by emotion.

I missed both my father's matches for Middlesex since they took place outside London during term time. Again, Wisden: in the Middlesex v Glamorgan match at Swansea in June 1949, he scored 18 and 2; later in the same month against Somerset (at Bath) he raised his batting average, with innings of 24 and 11. The Somerset match may be of some ironic interest to students of cricketing minutiae. Brearley, father and son, ushered in and out the Middlesex cricketing career of Fred Titmus. He made his debut that day at Bath and played his last match for Middlesex on 3 September 1976 at the Oval.

My first memories of first-class cricket date back to 1949 (when I was 7), the summer the New Zealanders toured England, and Jack Robertson scored 331 not out against Worcestershire. Robertson was my hero. I laid out my own little pitch in the back garden, mowed it and rolled it. I threw a tennis ball against the brick wall of the house, gripped my bat and played all the shots round the wicket: correct, precise (classical, I thought) and all in the manner of Jack Robertson.

Tom Scholar 'being' Thommo, and canine hazards for the batsman in Greenwich Park

1949: with sisters Jill and Margaret

Great fantasy matches came out of this. I was always Middlesex and I always arranged for Robertson, the opening bat, to get more runs even than Compton or Edrich. This seems interesting because Robertson was neither as spectacular as Compton nor as rugged and strong as Edrich. Yet I modelled myself after Robertson. I *was* Robertson. Robertson recently told me that in his boyhood fantasies he *was* Wally Hammond. A friend's son *is* Rodney Marsh. This idea of absorption into fantasy fascinates me.

At 10, I played in my first properly organized match. It took place at Middleton club near Bognor Regis. I was selected to play with a team of massive (to me) 16- and 17-year-olds against a colts side from Worthing. For the occasion, my aunt was asked to send a pair of white flannels from London. They arrived just in time. I went to bat at number 10 that day and I scored 5 not out. I can recall both shots: a cover drive that went for four and a little hook for one off slow bowling that seemed quick to me.

At 11, I scored my first century, 120 not out, against the Forest School. It earned me a gift I still cherish. The Rev C. J. Ellingham, senior English master at the school, presented me a copy of the MCC coaching book. On the fly-leaf is inscribed: 'Congratulations on your first hundred from one who never scored one but wishes he had.'

By then I was at the City of London School. Cricket does not play a large part in their games programme, partly because their playing fields are ten miles away. Yet, I was later coached by Reg Routledge, the former Middlesex all-rounder. My father taught me an orthodox Yorkshire approach. Reg got me to move my left hand more behind the bat and drag the bat down with it. The left elbow became less prominent. He kept saying, 'Let the ball come to you.'

At about 14, in a holiday match at Bognor, I faced a boy of about my own age, a boy already spoken of locally as a quick bowler. I scored two fours off his first over which pleased me greatly. The boy was John Snow, later of Sussex and England. My mother recently told me the epilogue to the story. As I hit my second four she overheard a spectator, who turned out to be John Snow's father, remarking that there was a boy who one day would play for England. John himself recently recalled the incident to a friend. 'Yes, Brearley,' he said, 'he was the bloke to get out.'

At school, meanwhile, I played the clarinet in the orchestra and took the part of Horatio in *Hamlet*. At 15 I had to decide what to do in the sixth form. I think I wanted to do something other than what my parents had done at University, maths. I went into classics, largely because I was good at it, it was well taught, and it seemed the respectable thing to do. Two years later, I won a scholarship to St John's College, Cambridge.

There I continued reading classics, and played the clarinet until a crucial rubber band holding down an inadequate pad broke early in a college concert. (The college organist left noisily after the first movement.) My acting career was also abortive: I had to give up a part in the Cambridge Greek play when I found out that the dates clashed with the University lacrosse match – though I did appear, in the evening performances only, as Hermes the *deus ex machina*, for the last two lines. I also kept wicket. At first slip was Eddie Craig, who later played for Lancashire, and now has returned to Cambridge as a philosophy don at Churchill College.

I used to ask Edward philosophical questions about freedom and minds. One of his party pieces at that time was to ask, 'Is the class of those classes that are members of themselves a member of itself?' I was impressed by his legerdemain, and also interested in the meatier questions. These conversations were one factor in my switching to philosophy in my third year. I realized that now what was beginning to interest me, apart from playing cricket, were things to do with people's minds. I can remember being stimulated along these lines at the tea parties of John Wisdom, the philosopher.

My cricket was helped a good deal by Cyril Coote, the groundsman at Fenner's. He had a deep belief in hitting through the ball with a straight bat, and would spend many hours throwing balls to us in the nets. He, like other Cambridge University employees, would call us young pups 'Sir' without in any way implying deference. One of his *mots* (about playing on a wet wicket) was, 'Get on the back foot, sir, and play it with a broomstick, sir.' Cyril, who had a game leg since he was 17, once scored 94 not out out of a total of 126 all out against Sidney Barnes who took all 10 wickets in the innings.

In my cricketing career at Cambridge I scored 4,068 runs, which is a record. I caused some modest stir when I bowled under-arm against Oxford and Sussex. The delivery is not revolutionary. Before 1835 under-arm bowling was mandatory in the game, and was last employed at Test level by G. H. Simpson-Hayward against South Africa in 1910. I didn't enter into the idea hastily. I practised. I had an under-arm stumping chance against Sussex. The batsman came down the wicket, missed the ball, and the wicket-keeper missed the stumping chance. It was a pity, it would have shut everybody up. I should have kept at it because there is no reason under-arm bowling shouldn't come back. It is a good, freakish variation if you are stuck.

In this account of the Ashes series, it perhaps is appropriate to mention that I first faced the Australians in my sixth first-class cricket match, when I scored 73 and 89.

After coming down from Cambridge with a first in Classics and a two-one in Moral Sciences, I enjoyed a rewarding year for Middlesex. I was named Young Cricketer of 1964. Nevertheless, I was uncertain about my career. I visited a department of the Civil Service and, largely because I was relaxed about the result, I came joint first in the Civil Service examination. I was given a year to decide if I wanted to join.

That autumn I was a member of the last MCC team to tour South Africa. After a reasonable start I lost form altogether. My trip was more rewarding in its broader aspects. I stayed on at the end of the tour, and met people from all political groups. I left South Africa cynical about the value of 'bridge-building' after these glimpses of the iniquities of apartheid. I joined the campaign, which arose over the d'Oliveira affair, to cancel the 1970 South African tour to England. Such a tour would have been an insult to coloured people in this country. Moreover, any marginal improvement of the situation in South Africa was, I felt, more likely to come from a policy of isolation in sport than in any other way. It seems to be working.

One more season, 1965, at Middlesex, and I returned to Cambridge as a student at St John's. I then accepted a place as a research assistant at the University of California which had a cricket interlude. I was, to my surprise, asked by the MCC to captain the Under-25 side that toured Pakistan that winter. We took out a strong side, including Knott, Underwood and Amiss, all my Test colleagues in later years. On that tour I had the highest innings score of my life, 312 not out, against the Northern Zone at Peshawar. The scorer is said to have thrown his pen away, overwhelmed, and walked off towards the Khyber Pass.

Despite that innings, and 223 the following week, I had no intention of playing cricket full-time. I wanted to be a philosopher. In 1968 I applied for, and got, a job lecturing at the University of Newcastle, and enjoyed it very much, keeping a hand in at cricket by playing an occasional match for Middlesex and in the Northumberland league for a former mining village, Percy Main.

Philosophy, as an academic profession, I finally found unfulfilling. While

Calmer days at Lord's: Middlesex *v* Glamorgan. We won this Championship match in early June. It was a Wednesday at Lord's, nice sunny day. Wicket-keeper is Eifion Jones, short leg Arthur Francis, umpire Peter Rochford. Photograph by J. H. Calvert

perhaps I was succeeding as a lecturer, and enjoying it, I felt I was contributing little as a creative philosopher. I felt I didn't have the peculiar drive needed to follow through intricate academic questions.

Once again, an opportunity opened. Middlesex asked me to captain the team. Why did I leave philosophy for sport? I suppose I am asked that question as often as I am asked what it feels like to bat against the fast-bowling of Jeff Thomson. The job of captaining a cricket team is challenging and stimulating, more than that description of cricket as 'chess on grass' might suggest. Chessmen move one at a time. There are more variables in cricket. Also, as captain of a team, you are responsible for a lot of group interaction and for getting the best out of people, not only for a short period of time but over the whole day, over the whole week, over the whole season.

My captaincy of Middlesex is well documented. We went from 16th place in the County League to sixth in my first year, won the Championship in 1976 and shared it last year with Kent. How long I will stay actively in cricket, I cannot say, but it is not something that fills my life. In recent years I have become interested in psychoanalysis and psychotherapy. When winter tours allow it, I have been working with disturbed adolescents at the Northgate Clinic in London and, again as I have time, doing courses in psychotherapy, a career I plan to pursue when my cricketing days are finished. There was little time for such study in 1977.

Gillette Cup Winners and Championship Winners (shared), 1977, Middlesex. Left to right: back row: D. Bennett (coach), Gould, Gatting, Emburey, Ross, Lamb, Daniel, Slack, Moulding, Tomlins, Butcher
Front row: Barlow, Selvey, Radley, Brearley, Smith, Featherstone, Jones, Edmonds.
Photograph by Bill Smith

3 The Common Enemy

The England team and selectors dine together on the eve of each Test match. On 15 June they gathered, with three MCC officials, at 7 o'clock for 7.30 in the committee dining room in the pavilion at Lord's. The room has a bar, two oils of nineteenth-century cricketing scenes, six oil portraits of early cricketing worthies, not least Benjamin Aislabie, who is remembered best for taking an MCC side to Rugby in Tom Brown's Schooldays. The fourth wall, leading onto a balcony, commands a view of the ground. According to custom, Graham Barlow, who was to make his first Test appearance in England, was seated beside Brearley. The meal: fresh vegetable soup, pâté de foie gras, grilled English sirloin steak, diced carrots, asparagus tips, garden peas, chips and new potatoes, apple pie with cream, a cheese board, 'After Eight' mints, coffee and tea. The drink was hock, beaujolais, port and brandy. Alan Knott chose to drink fresh orange juice and tea and honey. At 9 o'clock the selectors and MCC officials, having toasted and encouraged the players to join together, put aside the Packer Affair, and beat the common enemy, left the room. The players stayed on to discuss the forthcoming battle. It was a dinner to be repeated, in different places and styles, on the eve of each of the five Test matches.

I keep a log-book of my dreams beside my bed and on the morning of the Jubilee Test, which was my debut as a Test captain, I recorded two dreams. One took place near a hotel lift where I saw Tony Greig running down the corridor towards my room, perhaps to retrieve his things out of it. I trotted anxiously after him. The second dream took place in a small theatre where the actors on stage asked the audience to mime their own characters. The other members of the audience seemed uninhibited but I wondered what mime to perform. Finally I decided to be a shell with me peeping out.

When I consider these dreams I suppose they are easy enough to interpret. There is nothing unusual, for instance, in feeling a certain insecurity about such an exposed position as England cricket captain, and since all my Test matches had been played under Tony Greig, a powerful personality, the image of me anxiously trotting after him is not altogether out of place. As for coming out of the shell, the meaning of this seems clear enough, too.

We stayed at the Clarendon Court Hotel, near Lord's. On the first morning the sky over London looked grey and miserable. The report over the bedside radio predicted cloudy and damp weather, light drizzle, with late sunny spells and more rain to follow. It would not be a good day to bat. But if we didn't bat first, we might bat on an even worse wicket later in the match. Wind from the northeast. Unusual for Lord's. That would mean changing Bob Willis round to the nursery end, because he would prefer to bowl with the wind at his back. John Lever and Chris Old could bowl from the pavilion end. The temperature would be rather cool again. Knott would wear two sweaters and long johns. In all, the weather forecast suggested no clear-cut decision: it would be a toss you wouldn't mind losing.

I thought of the team dinner the previous evening. One thing about cricket is that you can plan your bowling much more than your batting. If the conditions help you, you bowl *your* way and largely dictate to the batsman. We discussed the batting order and key fielding positions and, in turn, the Australians. I think it was Derek Underwood who stressed that Australian batsmen were vulnerable – any good batsman was vulnerable – against quickish bowling on or just outside the off stump. This applies especially if the ball leaves the bat and, most especially, because a lot of Australians are on-side players. There were exceptions, of course, and one was Richie Robinson, the reserve wicket-keeper who might go in first. Robinson is an off-side player, but rather a wild one, and we decided to start off by bowling to that strength. If he became well-set, we could bowl more defensively at his middle and leg stumps.

Rick McCosker, the other opener, is very much an on-side player, who, because of his terrible jaw injury suffered against Willis in the Centenary Test, must be apprehensive about the bouncer. Craig Serjeant, who had scored a hundred against MCC the previous winter in Perth, is very quick to pull anything short of a length to square-leg or mid-wicket. We decided it would be wise to be careful about bowling short to him and bear in mind an extra fielder in the mid-wicket area.

Rain and sun at the Oval: One-day International. Chappell batting. Enjoyable farce. No one had seemed to know whether there was any provision for finishing the match next day if there was no finish; there was doubt as to whether all the streets near the Oval would be closed because of the Queen's Jubilee procession. So Chappell and I had agreed to play on whatever the weather. Australia had batted through some very bad light, so it was fair enough that we should stay out in this

Graham Barlow made the point that he had a chance of running out Greg Chappell because Chappell likes to take a single between mid-off and extra cover. I remember suggesting to Barlow that he might play cat-and-mouse games with Chappell and fiddle him out as, indeed, he almost had done more than once in the Prudential Trophy matches. Also, we agreed that Underwood to Chappell was a good thing. In the Centenary match he had bogged him down and eventually got him out to a wild, uncharacteristic shot.

Doug Walters is a dangerous attacking player and, although he had never done well in England, has an average of over 50 in Test cricket. It was noted that he likes slow bowlers. We fancied our chances against him if we could get the ball to move away from the bat, and use several slips and two gullies for as long as possible.

David Hookes, like Robinson, is vulnerable if you bowl to his strength, which is the off side. Christ Old added that he plays across his front leg so if the ball swings into him there is a chance of having him l.b.w. If Ian Davis played, we might get him out with extra lift, as Willis had done in the Birmingham Prudential match.

Rodney Marsh caused as much discussion as anyone. I was always amused by the sight (and even the mental image) of Rodney Marsh batting because I was reminded of Richard Scholar the three-year-old son of friends in South London. Richard modelled himself on the Australian: aggressive, his brother's green Cub cap tugged down, slamming away under the chestnut trees in Greenwich Park. 'I'm Rommarsh. Square-cut,' he'll say and he'll swing it to square-leg.

The real Marsh, however, is a formidable batsman; the last time he faced us in a Test he scored a hundred in the Centenary match. Old, who fancies left-handers, wanted to bowl against him. As for the field placing for Marsh, we wanted to have mid-off and mid-on very straight and leave cover open. He doesn't often hit the ball there, for a start, and the wide open space between mid-off and third man might encourage him to play a shot that's not natural to him.

There was a feeling that once you're past Marsh, you've reached the tail end of the batting and the hard work is over. Several people stressed, however, that Kerry O'Keeffe, Max Walker and Jeff Thomson could be dangerous. O'Keeffe, another on-side player, had played the new ball well at Melbourne. And in India we had learned the lesson that, although you aren't allowed to bowl bouncers at tail-enders it was important to make Thomson and Walker, both good drivers of the ball, realize you meant business. Willis, in particular, who has been hesitant to do this, was encouraged to dig a few in just short of a length to them.

As for Walker's bowling, Greig thought you could sometimes tell what he was bowling by the way he held the ball. When he bowled his leg-cutter, you could see his fingers were spread wider than when he bowled his in-swingers. Also, you might be able to tell which way he was trying to swing it by noticing

Left: Richard Scholar being Rodney Marsh. *Right:* Marsh at Manchester in a One-day International. Wham! We ended up with four or five men on the leg boundary, and he still hit the ball over or between them. It was high-quality butchery. *Below Right* shows Marsh during the Fourth Test

which side of the ball was shiny. I reckoned this wouldn't help me much. Even if you did notice it, there wasn't an awful lot you could do because the leg-cutter only occasionally gets a grip, so you've got to play it as a straight ball. While many players said they could spot the shiny side on a sunny day, most of us felt that looking for it would be a distraction.

Thomson was having trouble with his run-up and with no-balls that summer and, because of his shoulder injury, had taken it a little more slowly. He was a bit of an enigma. We honestly had no real idea how quick or short he would bowl. There was general agreement that the most dangerous thing about O'Keeffe was being caught bat–pad from his top-spinner. Len Pascoe, whom we had hardly seen, was almost two different bowlers in one: either very fast, with

Pascoe to Greig. Prudential match at Old Trafford. Greig got safely underneath the bouncer and has turned to watch Marsh take the ball. The position of the bat shows how one can, in ducking, instinctively push it up dangerously close to the ball. Walters nearly got out in this way. Tony is wearing the gloves he helped to design, made with a single piece of foam rubber to cover the four fingers and the back of the hand, the purpose being to spread the impact and lessen the chance of breaking a bone. They have helped me, I'm sure. This was the first time most of us had seen Pascoe. In this match he bowled very quickly, but rather wildly, in his tearaway vein lots of bouncers, or slower, to a fuller length. He is inexperienced. At a word from Chappell, he might switch from one style to the other between overs.

All in all, we were confident we could win the Ashes. We had won two of the three Prudential matches – preliminary skirmishes perhaps, but we reckoned we could get them out. We knew they had good bowlers and the crucial thing was to score enough runs. It would be hard work. Greig reminded us, as he often did: 'It's more of a sin to get out for forty than for nought.'

I was in a good frame of mind. I had just scored 123 not out against Hampshire, facing Andy Roberts, and it was clear the players were accepting me as captain.

Lying on my hotel bed, considering the details of the dinner, I suddenly thought, 'Oh, God, Geoff Miller!' In my comments round the table the night before, I had presumed that Barlow rather than Miller would play in the side. It was only a presumption, of course, because I was one of five selectors and no decision would be taken until just before the match. But I suppose, sitting there with the players, excited, imagining how my first Test as captain would go, this was an understandable mistake. In my own mind I had felt that we should play the specialist batsman, Barlow, rather than the all-rounder, Miller. Geoff must have noticed it. It was insensitive on my part.

After breakfast, which we had together in a separate room, I packed my bag with bits and pieces to take to the ground: Tolstoy's *Anna Karenina*, in case of rain or an early dismissal, a spare shirt, slippers for the pavilion, a couple of pens to write letters and sign autographs, and a pair of sunglasses.

The crowd that pressed round us at the Grace Gates, a full hour and a half before the match was to begin, sharpened the tension which is at its worst on the first morning of a Test match, especially the First Test. Apart from my anxieties about the game itself, there were other matters on my mind: parking the car, a misunderstanding with the Press over an alleged request for payment to players during a photo session the previous day at Lord's, collecting my complimentary tickets (which I usually give to my parents), the pitch, the final selection . . .

A package from a lady in Preston was in the dressing room. She said she loved watching cricket but couldn't stand the fact that we didn't wear bright white socks. So she had knitted twelve pairs to distribute to the team. (Since then, I've put mine in the wash with a green towel and they've come out greenish. I hope she's not disappointed.) As we changed someone commented that when Greig was captain everybody got a car, when Brearley was captain everybody got a free pair of socks.

Two other selectors, Ken Barrington and Charlie Elliott, joined me for a look at the pitch. No surprises: it was still slightly damp from water running down the hill under the covers. Lord's, especially when damp, likes the seam bowlers more than the spinners. This reinforced my idea that Geoff Miller should be left out. All four selectors agreed. In the dressing room I told Miller I was sorry about last night but, despite that lugubrious look of his, he took it well. No player likes being relegated to what we call 'the Catering Corps'. In fact, someone once said that the worst thing in the world is to be too good as twelfth man, because you might find you have that job for your whole career.

The Australians were out in the outfield, playing with their baseball gloves. They looked, generally, very athletic. The nets were not fit, but we went over to the nursery ground, and, while Barlow, Lever and Willis did their exercises and running, we did some catching of various sorts. One of the most important things about the Test series – and the winter series in India and the (spring) Centenary match, for that matter – was our extraordinarily high standard of close fielding, especially slip-fielding and wicket-keeping. Few catches went down. We attribute this in part to a drill we used in India and continued through the summer. A ball is thrown chest-high, from about fifteen yards, to a batsman, who steers or slices it towards a ring of slip-fielders, again about fifteen yards away. A slight technical difficulty about this is that you need lots of balls and boys fielding behind the slips.

Apart from simulating the real thing, this drill aids relaxation. Relaxed concentration is everyone's aim; I found an idea in a passage of Indian philosophy helpful for me, that one should not try to control the *outcome* of an endeavour, the outcome will take care of itself. So I try not to worry about whether the catch will stick, I think simply of relaxing, enjoying slip-fielding, and hoping the ball comes my way. In India I was also better as a slip-fielder for not having the responsibility of captaincy. Here again, there is a danger that worrying about the outcome (of a bowling change or a field-placing) spoils the result.

On the way back from that catching in the nursery ground I remember talking with Greig. 'I agree with what you said about getting out for 40,' I said, 'but, in your case, it is pretty important to give yourself a chance of getting to 40.'

It was now about 10.55 a.m., with the match due to begin at 11.30. Greg Chappell and I like to toss up early but, because there was still some uncertainty about the conditions, we waited. I used a 10p piece, although in later matches I used a Jubilee crown. I tossed it high. Chappell called 'tails', as he did all through the series. I won. I chose to bat.

4 The Two Ws: Woolmer and Willis

The First Test

Mike Brearley was the first top cricketer to wear a protective batting helmet. A polythene shell, resembling a scrum cap, it weighs only a few ounces, covers his vulnerable temple areas and fits snugly under his cricket cap. He and Tony Greig devised the idea during the summer of 1976 after facing the hostile West Indian Test bowling of Mike Holding and Andy Roberts. They visited the Nottingham firm which makes among other things protective headgear for children suffering from epilepsy. Both players, who, with Bill Swanwick who made it, applied for the patent on the product, had wax moulds made of their heads, but only Brearley followed it up with an actual helmet. 'Tony's head is about a foot higher off the ground than mine and therefore he's safer,' says Brearley. 'Also, as an opening batsman, I face more new ball bowling.'

As I walked through the Long Room, down the stairs and out onto the ground, it crossed my mind – of course it did – that this was my first match as Test Captain of England. We were playing for the Ashes. This was Lord's and people were watching me, as though through the cage of a zoo, and I was a little self-conscious in my helmet. I tried to put all these thoughts out of my mind and concentrate on opening the batting against the Australians.

For Middlesex, Mike Smith and I leave the question of who takes first ball in the lap of the gods; he goes to the near end each time. In the Tests, Amiss, as he usually does, took the first ball. That suited me, especially as I was interested to see from the non-striker's end how Thomson would start. He warms up differently from Dennis Lillee who exercises so hard in the dressing rooms that he comes onto the field in a sweat and straightway comes steaming in at you.

Thomson was loosening up with some short run-ups and practice balls to mid-on. I had already opened against him in four innings that summer and each time it had taken him a couple of overs to work up to full pace. This was different, though – a Test match, the real thing – and he might do something different.

Amiss took Thomson, whose first spell followed the same pattern as in the earlier matches, for the whole of the first over. I got Pascoe, who was coming in quick from the start, from the pavilion end. We began all right in the first forty minutes and then Amiss chopped the top of the stumps against Thomson's yorker: hit wicket although in fact given out bowled. Not long after, I got a nasty, lifting ball from Thomson and was caught off the glove at short leg for 9 So, we were 13 for two wickets, not an auspicious start.

Then we had a good stand, 98 runs in about two hours, between Woolmer and Randall. Randall played an exciting little innings with style and panache. By that time of year he already had a thing about getting out around 50. He would become jumpy and seek encouragement from his batting partners. As he approached his half-century we watched him on television in the dressing room. I remember somebody saying, 'Come on, Arkle. Concentrate. You've just begun. We're just beginning to get into a good position.' Then he played at a near-wide from Walker and was caught behind.

Greig came in at 111 for 3. He's an exciting batsman but unpredictable. Against the Indian spinners, he learned to build slow, controlled centuries. But when fast bowlers come racing in at him, his dander gets up. In recent Test matches, it is amazing how many times he has been bowled out by the fast bowlers, usually trying to drive. It's the Old Adam – he has to make things happen, stride high, assert himself, and smash an early four.

That's exactly what happened against Pascoe, who let loose a bouncer which Greig didn't pick up, and the ball hit him on the left shoulder. That stung Greig into retaliation. He immediately tried to hit back and, three balls later, Pascoe bowled him through the gate for 5.

Then there was a collapse: Barlow out for 1, Knott uncharacteristically caught at cover for 8. Old, Lever and Woolmer had also gone by the time we reached 189 for 9, and only a last wicket stand of 27 between Underwood and Willis hoisted us over the 200 mark. Woolmer, playing a mature innings, more or less ran out of partners, then ran himself out for 79.

The front-line Australian bowling looked very good. Though Thomson, bowling with the wind, hadn't quite worked up to full pace, he took four wickets. Walker was making the ball move and bounce very unevenly at the nursery end. Pascoe's pace was impressive. His action looked slightly unusual to me, facing him, and some of the other English batsmen thought so, too, but there certainly was not sufficient evidence to accuse him of throwing, as Ted Dexter did that weekend in the *Sunday Mirror*.

Bad light shortened the second day's play to 105 minutes, during which time the Australians scored 51 runs and John Lever took a wicket, bowling Robinson with a good in-swinger. Although not much cricket was played it was an interesting day. Willis started badly though he had behind him at the nursery end the brisk wind that had helped Thomson. He was getting his length and line wrong and bowled probably his worst spell of the series. Old and Lever bowled well, and in poor light and bitter weather McCosker and Chappell hung on grimly.

Chappell brought off a nice tactical ploy. When the rain began to fall late in the afternoon, he wouldn't allow the groundsman to cover the bowlers' follow-throughs. He wanted the game to be held up as long as possible once the rain let up so that there would be a shorter period of danger if Underwood bowled on a wet pitch. I objected: in English county cricket it has become standard practice

Top Left:
First Test. Early blow by Pascoe. He surprised Tony with this bouncer, which got up sharply and hit him on the left shoulder. Hookes (gulley), McCosker and Chappell (slips), Marsh, Robinson (short leg), Woolmer (non-striker)

Bottom Left:
Three balls later! Greig was half driving at it, the ball came down the hill and bowled him off his pad. It is amazing how often he has been out bowled by fullish-length balls from quick bowlers over the last couple of years. In between, of course, he has also scored a lot of runs

One of the special
commemorative
envelopes we signed
(this one supplied by
courtesy of Stamp
Publicity, Worthing)

to cover the bowlers' follow-throughs. I looked it up in the rules. Chappell was right. All that rainy afternoon, incidentally, I can remember signing hundreds of special commemorative envelopes celebrating the Jubilee Test match at Lord's.

On Saturday morning the pitch was damp, but the rain helped Underwood only marginally. We started with him from the nursery end. A fascinating duel with Chappell ensued, which Chappell won, but only just. Derek dropped a sharp caught-and-bowled chance, one that he would hold perhaps fifty per cent of the time. If that catch had stuck we would have had an excellent chance of bowling them out for less than our score. At the other end, Chris Old was bowling beautifully; he and Max Walker continually made the ball do remarkable things from the pavilion end throughout the match, but neither had much luck.

Chappell stuck it out. He batted for $2\frac{3}{4}$ hours before hitting a boundary. His on-drive against Underwood was risky when the ball held up a little, but since it is one of his best shots against him we put Randall at mid-on and Barlow at mid-wicket. When Randall went off with a bad elbow, Ealham, almost as good a fielder, replaced him.

Old had dismissed McCosker early on. Craig Serjeant took 40 minutes to get off the mark in his first Test. He played very well. His method of scoring against Underwood is unorthodox. He rarely off-drives, and on the on side he plays the ball square of mid-wicket and wide of mid-on, so we had these fielders much squarer than usual. When Derek bowled a slower ball, just outside off-stump, Serjeant lifted him to mid-wicket for 4. A risky shot, though he keeps his head still when he plays it. A few balls later, he did it again; another 4.

I suggested to Derek that we take a man from cover and put him at deep mid-wicket, to see if Serjeant would be tentative against the slower ball now that that area was closed. Serjeant seemed untroubled, and a couple of overs later he swept Underwood for another 4 from around middle-and-leg. Soon, Derek said he'd prefer to go back to his orthodox field; he would not bowl so many slower balls, and if Serjeant tried to hit him over mid-wicket, he might sky the ball off the top edge. We left mid-on and mid-wicket deepish and rather wide.

I mention this to point out the sort of games that go on; you try something out to see if it changes the way a batsman plays. It wasn't clear, to start with, whether we wanted Serjeant to play that shot or not. In the end we settled for letting him play it. In the second innings, as it turned out, he tried it once too often, being well caught by mid-wicket running back. He would not have

Serjeant batting at Lord's. An unorthodox but safe shot. He made us think a lot about our field-placing

played the shot if the man had been back, and might not have been caught if the on-side fielders had been closer, where they would normally be.

Serjeant and Chappell were going well when Willis bowled Chappell a bouncer, which he hooked for 4; next ball he drove without getting properly forward or over the ball, and was caught in the gulley for 66. 135 for 3.

Serjeant went from strength to strength. Walters went for his shots. I dropped him at slip off Woolmer when he was 21. It was bad weather for fielding, cold and gloomy, but the cricket was absorbing.

By five-thirty, Australia were 238 for 3, right on top. However, with the new ball Willis and Old struck back. Before lunch on the fourth day we had dismissed Australia for 296, a lead for them of only 80. Willis took 7 for 78, his best Test figures.

Bob has for years been the fastest bowler in England; but until the Indian tour he was very much a 'touch' bowler. He stayed fit in India. His 6 wickets for 40 at Calcutta gave him the confidence that he can get top players out even on slow wickets. Since Sydney, he has been running five miles a day, every day, except when he is bowling.

Technically, too, he has improved. Tony Greig persuaded him to alter his run-up. In the past, he rushed back and in like a runaway racehorse. He slowed that down, but lengthened his run-up. Most dramatically, he changed the angle of his approach from about 45 degrees to almost straight. As a result, he puts less strain on his body and the whole operation is more controlled, less frenzied. His

First Test, 1st innings. Woolmer pulls O'Keeffe for 4.

Bad ball, but very well struck. Woolmer is nicely balanced on his right foot, you can't pull or hook with both feet planted. Bob had worried a bit early in that first innings about the difficulty he had in scoring. We assured him he was doing well, that the runs would come. In the second innings he played his best-ever knock for England, a fluent 120.

One interesting thing about this picture is how vulnerable Robinson is at short leg. If that shot had been a bit lower, it could have hit him on the temple. Helmets for short leg fielders?

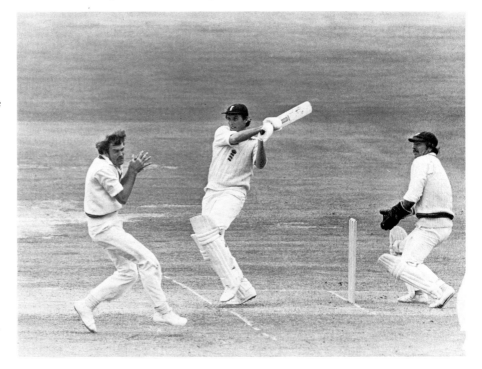

success is all the more pleasing as there is no more enthusiastic and hard-working team-man than Bob.

Our bowlers had given us the chance to save the game, but conditions still favoured seam bowlers. When Amiss was bowled by Thomson in the first over, our position was as gloomy as the weather. Woolmer and I were both dropped, but managed to add 132. After I was out for 49, Greig came in and played most responsibly, content to be second fiddle to Woolmer, until he reached his 100.

I cannot speak too highly of this hundred of Bob Woolmer's. He made batting look an agreeable pastime while I was struggling to stay in and Tony Greig was soon riding his luck. Bob had a very disappointing tour of India, in and out of

David Hookes at Lord's, sweeping Underwood. 2nd innings.

Woolmer is the biter bit, but he covers up much more safely than Robinson did. His hands have gone over the top of his head, so that his arms protect his face and head, and his knees and legs protect much of his body: a professional cover-up. Hookes has not quite rolled his wrists enough to keep the ball on the ground, though it landed well short of deep square-leg. Hookes never played an innings to compare with his 56 at Melbourne, but we bowled much better at him this series

the Test side. He got out repeatedly after reaching 15 or 20, often against rather ordinary medium-pacers. Against the spinners there, on pitches that helped them, he seemed rather ponderous, a buzzard mobbed by small birds.

In England, against quicker bowling on firmer pitches, he started the season marvellously. He forced his way into the side for the First Test (having been left out of the One-day Internationals), by sheer performance. He has all the shots, and time to play them. Perhaps his rather placid temperament needed the sting of failure for him to become aggressive and greedy for runs. It is difficult

I had decided that I was going to enjoy myself as captain of England, for however long it lasted. Photograph by courtesy of the *Daily Mail*

otherwise to account for the change, except, as is so often the case, by reminding ourselves of the importance of luck. He played-and-missed, rather than edged, early on. He was dropped, whereas in India he seemed to make no more mistakes but each was fatal. In the short run, the margin between success and failure is slight, both for individuals and for teams.

He is an excellent man to have in the side, utterly reliable, professional and helpful.

He was at last fourth out at 263. We were now 183 runs ahead, with only four and a half hours left of the match. Surprisingly, both sides had slight chances of winning from this position, Australia when they took the last 6 wickets for 42, England when we took the first 5 wickets for 71, several of them from over-ambitious shots. In the end, though, too much time had been lost because of rain and bad light to make a result possible.

The Test ended with honours even. We came in the end quite close to winning, but for most of the match, we had been fighting to earn a draw. The game underlined what we knew before, that each side was stronger in bowling than in batting. At this point the Australians must have had as much reason for confidence as we had. But we knew that as well as those who played at Lord's, Geoff Boycott had announced that he was available for selection, and Mike Hendrick was in great form.

Personally, I was fairly happy. I had decided that I was going to enjoy myself as captain of England. It is of course an honour which comes to few players; many of these lose their *joie de vivre,* being worn down by the pressures of the job. Not long after the Lord's Test I played against Ray Illingworth in a John Player League match at Lord's. I asked his opinion about players around the country, and invited his comments on the First Test. He said he wondered if I should have tried bowling Bob Willis from the pavilion end at some stage. Of course this had crossed my mind; but switching him would have meant breaking his rhythm, and having him bowl into the wind. Ray also said that he had learned, as captain of England, that it was most important not to worry too much about losing the job. A few weeks earlier, the idea of getting the job, much less losing it, had not occurred to me.

5 Tracing the Call

On the 1976–77 tour of India and Australia, Brearley played well and seemed in a fair position to retain his place as vice-captain under Tony Greig for the forthcoming battle for the Ashes against Australia. But Kerry Packer, the Australian television tycoon, rebuffed by the Australian Cricket Board in his bid to televise matches, had signed Greig and enlisted him to recruit top England players in a series of matches, later called Super-Tests. Consulting his diary and journals, Brearley later looked back on the unfolding drama:

20 March, Sydney, Australia: the Sunday after the Centenary match. The first scent that 'something big' might be in the air came when four of us who had stayed on in Australia (Greig, Willis, Barlow and myself) were entertained to a barbeque. The host, Dr Arthur Jackson, treated many Australian sportsmen not only physically but through hypnosis. He had been talking to Willis, a notoriously bad sleeper, about the uses of hypnosis in relaxation and gave him cassette tapes which Bob used through the summer to induce sleep.

Greig spoke that day to Willis about general fitness. It seemed at the time a familiar theme because Greig and I had worked hard with Bob on fitness through the India tour. But this time Tony hinted at a new highly-paid circuit in Australia. If 'Goose' could manage 7 overs at a time, fast, rather than 5; and 6 in his second spell, equally fast, rather than 3, there was no limit to the money he might make. It did not occur to me then, though, that such a circuit would clash with Test cricket. Willis was equally unaware of the scale of the proposal.

23 March. Flew from Sydney to London with Willis, in seats with extra leg room to accommodate him, and read the book *The Van Aaken Method* by Dr Ernst van Aaken, who believes that fitness and health are only possible if you run for at least half an hour a day. This is beneficial to a bowler, especially to a fast bowler such as Willis. For me, running is a tedious proposition. My exercising is mostly stretching, which we often did with Bernard Thomas in India.

9 May. The Bomb dropped: the Packer proposal was revealed in the Press; apparently there was a leak. The intention was that the news should break during the First Test at Lord's.

11 May. Middlesex played Kent in a county match at Lord's. I learned more of the Packer plan from Knott and Underwood, who were by then being pilloried in the Press as renegades, traitors and defectors to the enemy camp. Both stressed the fact that Packer was offering them and their families a security that they could never get from Kent or England. They knew that injury or loss of form (or favour) could easily mean no Test cricket; (in fact, last summer was the first in which Derek had played in all the home Tests). Knott pointed out that there was not even any guarantee that an MCC tour would take place in the winter, since there was political trouble in Pakistan.

Both hoped that a compromise would be reached such that they could play for England as well as for Packer but, if not, they were prepared to accept the consequences. I told Derek I thought he had made a mistake if he had done anything which jeopardized his county career, which had after all been the fulcrum of his life since he was 17. He, Knott, and Asif Iqbal had just met the Kent chairman, who assured them that Kent would not want to take any action against them since their Packer contracts were for a period outside the months covered by their county contract.

13 May (a Friday). The announcement was made that Tony Greig was sacked as captain of England. The news broke in the afternoon. I was staying with friends in Greenwich, and had just got back from Lord's where the match with Kent had been abandoned. The phone rang. The *Daily Mirror* wanted a comment from the vice-captain on this dramatic dismissal only 34 days before the First Test against the Australians. My very first reaction was panic. For a minute I thought 'I don't want the job. I just want to play. Should they have sacked Greig?' I asked for a half hour to collect my thoughts. I put out a statement to the Press Association saying (honestly) that I regretted that Tony should lose the captaincy after doing so fine a job on tour. By then, though, I was calmer, and happier about the prospect. If Tony couldn't do it, I was probably the next best. I had the respect of most county cricketers both as batsman and captain, and especially of those who had been on the tour. I began to relish the idea, though of course some nervousness remained.

14 May. I travelled to Kent with friends where, at a bird sanctuary, I saw and heard nightingales for the first time in my life.

24 May. Visited a teaching psychoanalyst to discuss when I might start part-time training as a psychoanalyst, which could be started while I was playing cricket but not, of course, while I was on winter tour.

25 May. On the first day of the MCC *v* Australians match at Lord's, Donald Carr, secretary of the Test and County Cricket Board, said that they would like me to captain England in the One-day Internationals; but that before I was officially appointed he wanted some sort of assurance from me *vis-a-vis* Mr Packer. Naturally, they did not want to be in the process of building a new side only to find in the Press that a second captain had abandoned the crew. Ideally, he would like me to say that I would not join Packer while I was captain; I was not prepared to promise this, but I was willing to say that if I did seriously consider joining, I would first discuss it with Donald Carr or the Chairman of Selectors, Alec Bedser. I could understand why they felt Greig had broken their implicit trust. My answer was satisfactory. The next morning my appointment was made official and public.

I noted in my journal at this time that it was characteristic of Greig that he should refer to his captaincy as 'a reign'. I would not, implicitly or explicitly, refer to myself as king, or talk of '*my*' team.

The whole story has epic, almost mythological elements in it that I find fascinating. Tony Greig, the Prince Charming, the Golden Giant who comes from afar (South Africa) to set to rights our tottering State (English cricket). Like Oedipus (without the limp) he rids the State of the bane that sits upon its walls (we win in India). Does he, now, outreach himself by challenging the gods? Is this his hubris? Prometheus, who stole fire from the gods for men, spent many years chained to a rock in Asia Minor with an eagle pecking at his liver; Greig's banishment will not, we presume, be as uncomfortable, though I do like the image of him playing Faustus to Mr Packer's Mephistopheles.

Is Greig, in this egregious melodrama, Prometheus or Satan? Alan Knott said that Greig has done more for the professional cricket than any other man. Alex

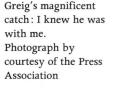

Greig's magnificent catch: I knew he was with me.
Photograph by courtesy of the Press Association

Bannister, on the other hand, said that Greig *et al.* were 'selling out the game that has made them'.

Taking on the whole power-structure, the Establishment of whatever sort, *is* the matter of a myth. Within each of us, such an act resonates with our own deep feelings about power, obedience and revolt. One aspect of my feeling, I admit, was admiration for one who would dare so far. 'How should I presume? . . . I shall measure out my life in coffee spoons.'

Another thought in this area of myth was what role did I play? It occurred to me that I was like the Chorus Leader in the Greek plays, analysing the fate of the city, waiting and watching; though also, I know, playing my part. I wondered if, at first, I viewed myself as a stop-gap until a new King emerged. The chorus leader is a leader, but not a charismatic king. I didn't entirely like this modest image, but I recognized myself in it. And I did not feel inclined to say 'In my reign as England captain . . .'

2 June. First Prudential Trophy match at Old Trafford. While these thoughts were inchoate somewhere deep in my mind, one nearer the surface was the apprehension over how Greig would respond, especially as he had just been kicked out as captain. As luck would have it, a very low, sharp chance came to Greig in the second or third over. He dived and caught it left-handed and held his hand up high. It gave him an early opportunity to show that he was with me, still dead-keen for England.

Tony Greig and I, absorbed in the job in hand.
Photographs by courtesy of the *Daily Mail*

6 The Struggle Against Chappell

The Second Test

The Sun *carried the headline 'Toss this Pitch Out' on 7 July, the morning of the opening day. 'Old Trafford's chequered Test match history could come to a sudden end unless the wicket behaves much better than in recent years.' Tony Greig told his ghost-writer at the newspaper, 'If there is any repetition of the debacle we suffered last year, I believe Manchester should be eliminated from the Test Match circuit.' Greig reviewed the erratic Test history of Old Trafford, from the 'spinners' paradise' in 1956 when Jim Laker took 19 wickets, to the 'harrowing sights' of John Edrich and Brian Close nearly being badly injured the previous summer by the West Indian fast bowlers. Generalizing, he blamed groundsmen all over the country (who, he thought, were both underworked and underpaid), modern machinery and modern top-dressings. He called for the return of 'old-fashioned muscle power' to save Old Trafford. It was at Greig's instigation that the pitches at Hove had been so radically improved in the previous two years. Other newspapers also expressed concern over the wicket, pointing out that Old Trafford's newly-appointed groundsman had left his job only a few weeks before the Test. Greig, who did not write the provocative headline, was later officially reprimanded by the Test and County Cricket Board, and his county, Sussex, fined £500 for authorizing publication of the article.*

Greig was writing about Old Trafford in general, not about this pitch in particular, as he had not seen it. By the time we had seen it, when we went to the ground to practise, many of our fears were allayed. It was flat, dry, and relatively grassless. There were cracks at the Stretford end. Greig picked up a rumour that, because of the pitch, Australia planned to leave out Pascoe for Bright.

Over dinner we discussed the rumour. We could hardly believe it. After our experience in India we now backed ourselves in a spin-contest against anyone in the world. Moreover Pascoe had taken five wickets at Lord's and was rapidly improving. In the event, they were to miss him crucially, because throughout the match a strong breeze blew straight down the pitch from the railway end, helping the quick bowlers. What is more, the pitch had more bounce than we expected. As a result neither side could afford to bowl many overs of spinners into the cracked end, so it deteriorated very little. Chappell, therefore, was unable to keep the pressure on our batsmen without Pascoe to support Thomson.

Chappell's team was *his* problem. Chappell himself was one of ours and much of our continuing tactical discussion concerned ways of getting him out. 'All the other Australians seem a bit dodgy when they start,' said Willis, 'but Chappell seems in control.' We reviewed Chappell's innings at Lord's: Willis got him just after bowling a bouncer and, in the second innings, he was out trying to pull Old. Amiss put a point to Willis. 'When you bowl to him, Bob, you seem a different bowler. After one early bouncer, he knows he won't get any more, so he moves confidently onto his front foot.' Amiss then added, with the relish of a man who has received his share of intimidatory bowling. 'All top batsmen go through a period of timidity sometime in their careers. Give him a bombardment. See how that affects him.'

Knott agreed with the idea. He felt it was worth the risk of a few boundaries to make Chappell play differently. I agreed, too, providing there was pace in the pitch and Bob was happy with the idea. His agreement was crucial. I remember John Lever saying to me at Melbourne that he does not like to be *told* to bowl a bouncer, he has to *feel* right to make it worthwhile. Furthermore, I didn't want to endanger Willis' confidence, which had grown further with his nine wickets at Lord's. Only six months before, in India, he told me he wished he had Chris Old's ability. I told him then that Chris had *different* ability and he had plenty himself. Finally, I did not want Willis to lose his rhythm or his usual line and length by trying too hard to bowl flat-out and short. Was Bob happy with the plan? Willis was happy. This line of attack against Chappell could of course misfire. Underwood stressed the need to keep him on a tight rein, as we had at Melbourne and Lord's.

It was in all a successful dinner. At Test level, every player has useful ideas to contribute to a tactical discussion and, by contributing, each feels he is part of the team. I don't take credit for these open discussions because they had begun in India, but I think it is fair to say I have made them even more open.

A Test match occupies a week of one's life and it is important that the players should be comfortable. Many of us were tired, having had little rest since landing at Bombay the previous November. It was hot, too, and although I insist on catching practice, my policy is to leave it to the players to set their own limits of practice before a match. In the heat that day, practice was short, and to combat the heat in the hotel, where there was no air-conditioning, Knott had an answer. Fill your bath with cold water, he said, and stand in it now and again through the night. I took his advice. I also had started a collection of tapes and, for the first time, I could listen to some of my favourite music, in my room.

I drove to the ground with my Middlesex colleague, Graham Barlow, who saw a car with the registration number GDB, his initials, and two minutes later we saw one with the number JMB, mine. He felt it was a good omen for us both. The remark made me feel uneasy, since I thought it unlikely that Barlow would play. In the event, he was replaced by Miller, the only change from the side that had played at Lord's. The rumour about Pascoe was right. Pascoe and Robinson were dropped for Bright and Davis.

Chappell's call was right. In the baking heat, it was a good toss to win. Willis bowled well and, finding a good, shortish length, felt no need for the intimidatory bouncer. It was Greig, bowling out-swingers to a defensive field, who finally had Chappell caught behind for a graceful 44.

Doug Walters was the man who caused trouble that day. He came in with Australia 96 for 3 and, with Marsh taking the supporting role much of the time, left at 246 for 7 wickets. I always feel you need about sixteen fielders when Walters is batting. He plays strokes all round the wicket and if you keep too many close-fielders he can have 30 or 40 before you can blink. We started with five up, three slips and two gullies. He scored some early fours. When I took away third slip, he edged a four in the air through the space between second slip and gulley. In general, we found that once we needed to post a mid-off, the slip cordon was weakened so much that we often needed a third man as well. Sometimes this meant a rather sudden transition from attack – with five in the slip ring – to defence with only three.

By six o'clock Marsh and Walters had put on 98, we were getting ragged, the ball was soft, they were 238 and looking like reaching 400. I tried Miller, who earlier in the day had bowled one nervous over. He bowled an off-spinner, pitching outside Marsh's off stump, in the rough that was already beginning to powder. Marsh, trying to hit to long-on, skied to Amiss and ten minutes later Walters, a superb player of spinners, hit a full-toss into Greig's hands at extra cover. By just after 1 p.m. on Friday, Australia were 297 all out.

In the twenty minutes before lunch, Thomson got on top of us. He had just been batting, and this time he came in fast from the start. He hit Amiss on the shoulder. I mostly was having an awkward time against Walker, always a tough customer, and soon after lunch we were both gone: me for 6, caught at slip, playing tentatively off Thomson; Amiss for 11, attempting to hook Walker.

Left: A nice picture of Greg Chappell playing a characteristic shot off his hip. We often had a man at backward square-leg especially for this shot and occasionally had him close in case he hit in the air a little way. There's no name for this shot. Greg plays it with a straight bat off a ball from a fastish bowler from around leg-stump or middle-and-leg. Very few batsmen can play it – most people are just nudging it round the corner, but he plays it there with a free flow of the bat. Notice the upright balanced position, no tendency to fall over towards the off side. He's tall – about 6′ 2″ – and on his toes, so that even if the ball bounces a bit more than usual he can still play it down from say, waist height. He is very much a 'sideways-on' player, that is, he generally keeps his left side facing down the wicket towards the bowler; in this shot, we can see that just after he's hit the ball his left side is facing behind square-leg, so that from his initial position he has swivelled through an angle of more than 90°. I remember him playing this shot at Lord's off balls from Lever and Old that were good balls, moving in to him down the slope, and he still had time to play this forcing shot when most of us would have been glad to get a thick edge to fine leg for one. The man who played this shot as well as Chappell, and similarly, was Sobers. Amongst Englishmen, only Amiss has it as a stock stroke, and he's not so tall, so he can't play it as well when the ball bounces. I think this shot of Chappell's impresses the players more than the public because we know how hard it is to play. Anyone can play the odd off-drive or late-cut that look good. To say, though, that it is a professional's professional shot implies too little, it suggests a workaday, bread-and-butter shot, and this is more than that. It's very central to my image of Chappell.

Old Trafford: 'Have a bowl, Dusty!' Miller got 3 important wickets in this Test, though he was nervous to start with and was lucky to get Walters. I maintain that I was right to use him as sparingly as I did

In the dressing room, Amiss was gloomy and worried. He also had lost some confidence and was walking around seeking advice from everybody on how to play quick bowling. I didn't want to discuss his technique at that point. I wanted to think about my own.

What I had done wrong, I decided, was fall between two stools. I had not stayed inside the line of the ball and let it go, nor had I got right into line with the ball.

Woolmer driving (at Old Trafford). A characteristic forcing shot without any extra flourish. He hasn't come far forward to drive, especially as it's obviously Bright or O'Keeffe bowling. His head is nicely placed, absolutely steady watching the ball. His arms have broken a little in the follow-through but the bat has not gone right over his shoulder as it would do with someone who really hits rather than strokes the ball. If we changed the face, this could be a younger Colin Cowdrey. Marsh does not have the same legs-together technique as Knott; but the fingers point down and there has been no tendency to close the hands too early

Greig drives O'Keeffe
for 6 over long-off.
Tremendous shot.
Tony leans back
slightly to give it
everything

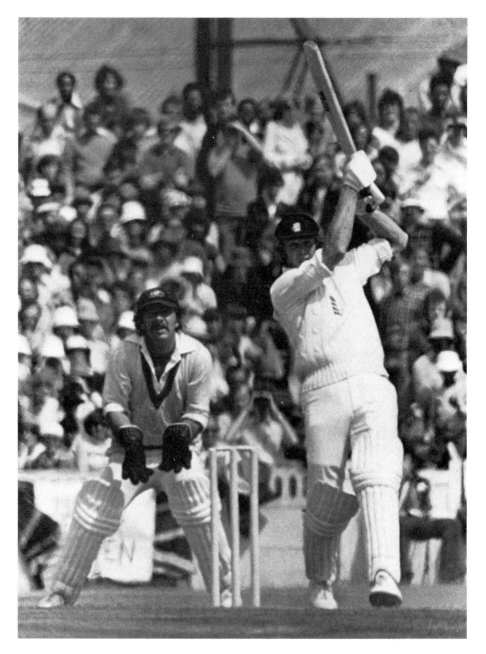

On the field, however, our position was improving. Although Thomson and
Walker were bowling perseveringly and well, they were getting indifferent
support through dropped catches. Superb batting by Woolmer, Randall and
Greig enabled us to score 436, a lead of 139. At one stage, when the score was
325 for 3 we were hoping to reach a total in the region of 500.

That Sunday, Geoff Boycott, scoring 76, led Yorkshire to a fine win over

Lancashire in the televised Sunday League match. He was given a hero's welcome by the Headingley crowd, a foretaste of what was to come and, as I watched in my hotel room, a vivid reinforcement of my certainty that he belonged in the England side.

On Monday morning, much refreshed, I arrived early. I was not sorry to see that the rough, produced especially by Willis and Walker, now stretched a long way down the pitch at the Stretford Road end, quite close to the leg stump. My mind went back to a conversation I had many years ago in the old Sind Club in Karachi.

Intikhab Alam and I had signed the visitors' book, ordered drinks and sat in one of those big, panelled rooms that remain from the Empire. Intikhab, bowling round the wicket, an unorthodox delivery for him, had troubled us.

He had given much thought to the tactic. The benefits of such a ball bowled into the rough are, of course, that a batsman has trouble judging both the height and the sharpness of its turn. The thing you must not do, he said, was bowl on off-stump or outside off-stump, because the ball already was coming across the batsman and he would have extra room to play his shots. Intikhab was clear that you must have more of your fielders than usual on the leg side, and we went through some of the possibilities in detail. Ever since then, I have felt that this line of attack could profitably be used more often than it is.

That morning, I asked Knott what he thought Derek Underwood's response would be to the idea of bowling over the wicket. Knott has played in almost every one of Underwood's matches over several years past. He was not encouraging. 'Deadly doesn't like his fields tampered with,' he said. 'He likes them orthodox. Also, the last time I remember him bowling over the wicket was during the MCC tour of India and Pakistan in 1972–73. Norman Gifford was much better in this style, and Underwood was left out for the next Test.'

After my net, I talked with Derek about the possibility of him bowling over the wicket and what fields he might have. There wouldn't be that much risk because he could always come back round the wicket. I wanted him to get excited about bowling over the wicket to Chappell. I'd like an extra man on the leg side. I drew it on an envelope and, as we talked, he became enthusiastic.

By the end of that day, Derek had taken 6 for 66 in 32.5 overs. He took three of these wickets bowling over the wicket to right-handers. It would be wrong to think that this tactic won us the match, since, by the time he was bowling this way we already had 4 second innings wickets, and the Australians were still behind our score. However, from a psychological and technical point of view, it was for me one of the most interesting episodes in the series.

When we went into the field soon after the start, Willis gave himself an early opportunity to try his new hostility towards Chappell by having McCosker caught off a mis-hook for 0. He now had dismissed McCosker for 1, 2 and 0 in his last three Test innings. Willis whistled the second ball past Chappell. Soon, Chappell hooked him for six just over Lever's head at long leg. On any other

Walters l.b.w. Greig 10 at Old Trafford. Second innings, last over before lunch, fourth day. I brought Tony on just for this over. Underwood had been bowling from this end, into the wind. Walters is a superb player of spinners, and we were thinking that it would be nice to have an over of someone quicker at him. Willis was, I think, bowling from the other end; Old had had several overs, and anyway was not quite at his best; Lever had not looked too fiery into this strong wind. So the ideal man, with his extra aggression and his ability to cut through the wind and still get bounce, was Greig. He said he'd bowl him a bouncer early in the over, which he did, second ball. There are three reasons for this; one is that though Doug can hook well, he does hook in the air, especially early in his innings. Secondly, he is much more likely, at this stage, to duck, but then as he ducks, his bat goes up above his head like a periscope. John Snow got him caught off the periscope like this several times in earlier series, and we narrowly missed doing so fifteen or twenty times in this one. The third reason for the bouncer was to produce exactly this effect; next ball he went back instead of forward to a ball of fullish length that came back off the seam from the off. It has struck him on the roll of the right pad, in front of about middle-and-off stumps – plumb l.b.w. Tommy Spencer is about to give him out with his right hand. We can see how 'square-on' he's got, with his right foot pointing down the wicket, and he's fallen across to the off, finishing up well outside the off stump. I think it was Greiggy's idea that he should bowl, and that he should try the bouncer. The pundits were saying 'This is Underwood's pitch, why on earth take him off for one over, and why Greig in his place?' – it's gratifying when something comes off like this. And Walters was very much a danger-man, he'd scored a fine 88 in the first innings.

ground, he would probably have been out, but the boundary here is unusually short. Two overs later, in Willis' words, 'I sat him on his backside, and he made a bit of a meal of getting up'.

Underwood started round the wicket. Chappell on-drove him for two fours (at this point we missed Barlow in the field), and took 21 off two overs. Derek was bowling too full a length and too much towards leg-stump. He was 'pressing' anxiously. In fact he had only taken 16 wickets so far this season. John Woodcock said that 'it is not unreasonable to wonder whether he was being unsettled by the reaction to his Packer signing'. At this point he had a stroke of luck. Serjeant turned him off the face of the bat and Woolmer caught a brilliant reflex catch at short leg.

Greig again took a vital wicket, that of Walters, just on lunch-time, when Australia were 92 for 4.

After lunch Hookes played well. Australia were ahead of us still with 4 wickets down when Miller got Hookes. It was, I think, during this stand that Underwood started to bowl over the wicket to the right-hander. Several times we had, mutually, hesitations about the appropriate field. When he has to depart from orthodoxy, Derek can be surprisingly uncertain, for so great a bowler, about what field he wants. At those times it is tempting for the captain to take over. I remember feeling sorry for Derek once or twice in India, as he stood, covered with sweat and dust, at the back of his run-up, feet turned out and trousers sagging like a cricketing Chaplin, while Greig directed fielders this way and that. But when I became captain, I could also see how Greig felt, that if he didn't take charge completely the ship would be quite directionless.

I was prepared to risk moments of indecisiveness for the sake of involving Derek more in the strategy.

Technically, the problems are interesting. A left-arm slow bowler, coming over the wicket, usually needs a slip, a mid-off, extra cover, and square cover, on the off side. On the leg side, he must have a backward square-leg, deepish but not right out, for the mis-hit sweep. He needs a short square-leg, and a mid-on. One other fielder must be behind square on the leg side, either at short leg or back twenty yards if the batsman is looking to sweep. The last fielder should probably be at mid-wicket, though one might be able to leave that area open to encourage the on-drive against the viciously spinning ball, in which case he can go to gulley or silly point or short extra cover. Great flexibility is needed; and one is automatically involved in agreeable cat-and-mouse games, since good players will alter their play depending on where one has the close catchers.

Fortunately, no one stayed too long with Chappell. Marsh was caught at mid-on, Bright caught and bowled. O'Keeffe, as usual, was difficult to shift. Gradually, though, we, and Underwood in particular, slowed Chappell down. His second fifty took 128 balls, while his first took only 68. He received another 34 balls while scoring his last 12 runs. At last, trying to make room to force Underwood through the off side, he edged a ball into his stumps.

Another important moment at Old Trafford. Chappell b. Underwood 112. The first thing to notice in this picture is that Underwood is bowling over the wicket, into the rough just outside the leg stump (obscured by the bowler). We can see from where Knott's hands are that the ball would have just missed off-stump, so it probably pitched around middle-and-leg. Chappell has stepped back to give himself room to hit the ball on the off side. The ball kept low, and he got an inside edge. It wasn't a particularly good ball, a bit shorter than Derek would have liked; but as often happens, he had earned the wicket by what went before. Chappell was getting a bit fidgety about how he was going to score. With O'Keeffe at the other end they had taken the score, slowly but importantly, from 147 for 7 to 202. It had been a stubborn stand, we needed the breakthrough, and above all we needed Chappell out. In fact, he did not get another 50 in the series.

The picture shows how wide I get at slip for Derek. Obviously I stand much wider when he bowls over the wicket, though he likes to have me unusually wide at all times. I had just gone wider, because I felt that Chappell might try to steer the ball through the gulley area. Woolmer is in his usual position, full crouch, head still, watching the roll of the batsman's pads. He had earlier caught a marvellous reflex catch there to get rid of Serjeant.

This picture also shows a lot about Alan Knott's technique. One of the reasons he does all his exercises is that he believes it's important to be able to take a ball around his ankles without bending his knees, and with his legs together (as they almost are in this picture). Then, if he misses the ball with his hands, it shouldn't go for byes. What's more, if the edge beats his gloves, there's no knee or elbow sticking out to obscure first slip's view, or to stop the ball. I had never appreciated this before I went to India in 1976–7 and caught several catches at slip off Derek Underwood. Not once was my view impeded by Knotty's body. He needs, therefore, to stretch his hamstrings constantly, and his neck is always under pressure, to look up towards the bowler. He had two car accidents a couple of years ago, since when he has had a lot of trouble with his neck. It is surprising how many spectators write in complaining of Knott's apparently gratuitous exercising; they're wrong, I'm sure.

This ball virtually ensured that we would win the match, and also put an end to the possibility that Chappell might cut loose and really dominate.

O'Keeffe hooks Greig at Manchester. Not particularly graceful, but effective. We only got O'Keeffe out twice in six innings, each time hooking at Willis. He was not much troubled with this bouncer from Greig. He plays straight in defence and limits himself to the shots he can play

Chappell pulls Lever for 4. He has played this in front of square. Though the hands have come over the ball, it looks as if the ball may have gone in the air

Thomson to Amiss. Fifth day, Old Trafford. Dennis has got into position to play the ball, seen it 'get big' on him, and withdrawn his head and taken his right hand off the bat. Though he has taken his eye off the ball, he is not in great danger of getting hurt since it is the back of his shoulder that is most likely to be hit. Even that's not ideal, however. What's more, if he is late and the ball is straighter, he can get hit on the back of his head as he was by Michael Holding in MCC *v* W. Indies match 1976. This was Thomson's most hostile bowling of the whole series. I don't look too cheerful at the other end.

Chappell, at slip, as usual stands a little wider than I do. This is discussed on page 68.

The wear on the pitch, and Underwood's foot marks bowling over the wicket, can be seen. Underwood bowls from much closer to the stumps when he bowls over the wicket than when he bowls round.

After Chappell, the innings folded quickly but his was a memorable performance, one of the best I have ever seen. Yet it may be that, crazy as it sounds, the way we handled Greg Chappell at Old Trafford represented a tactical and psychological victory; certainly he did not score another 50 in the series.

England then needed 79 for victory and, towards that victory, I contributed 44, my most satisfying innings of the series.

When I was out, Charlie Elliott, one of the selectors, said to me, 'Well played, bad luck. But if it's some consolation, you've got plenty more chances of batting. We want you to captain the next three Test matches.' That was when I learnt of the appointment, but I'll never forget straight after the match, after the

Bright to Brearley. Fifth day, Old Trafford. Bright, following Underwood, is bowling over the wicket, though from the other end. The wear on the pitch is visible. Amiss, Marsh and I are all playing in crepes; I feel more comfortable when I can bat without spikes. My hands are apart on the handle; I have found over the past two or three years that I get more control this way without losing driving power. The ball bounced high, judging by Marsh's reaction

champagne on the balcony, I went over to the television platform high above the ground. I was climbing up the ladder, hand over hand, trying to avoid crashing to my death, and when I got about three rungs from the top an announcement came over the loud speaker. 'Mike Brearley has been appointed Captain for the rest of the series.'

7 Thomson Concentrates the Mind Wonderfully

Brearley's Innings in the Second Test

Brearley's bat is out of the ordinary, though hardly revolutionary, and is cut from a special willow-grove in Essex. Perimeter-weighted (i.e. the back is gouged out rather like a heel-and-toe style golf club), it weighs 2 lb 8 oz, about two ounces more than average among top-class players. Its centre of gravity is nearer the grip than most bats, a balance which accommodates his notably erect pick-up action. The lower, right-hand half of the rubberized grip is double-thickness. This not only prevents jarring but, Brearley feels, dissuades him from clasping his bat too tightly with his right hand. 'Mike times the ball so well he is very good on bats,' say Gray-Nicolls, his batmaker, 'he has two bats going for a season whereas some vicious sloggers get through eight or nine.'

The first thing most cricket followers ask me is what it is like to bat against such out-and-out fast bowlers as Holding, Roberts, Daniel, Lillee, Pascoe and Thomson. My short answer is 'exciting'. The adrenalin is pumping, you are alert and, as Dr Johnson said about the man who faces hanging, 'it concentrates his mind wonderfully'.

Thomson was bowling with more hostility that second innings at Old Trafford than he did all summer – angrily, as if expressing all the frustration of a side about to lose in England for the first time in fourteen Tests. He looked hostile, too. He's known as 'Two-Up' among the Australian players, because at times he has given two fingers to the crowd. You know you're in a contest.

Coming in only a few minutes before close of play both hinders and helps a batsman. The most dangerous part of an innings is when you start and, over two days, you obviously start twice. On the other hand, you can see the end, you know how long you have to stick out. I don't mind going to the crease after a long time in the field, however, because I'm relaxed and play a bit more freely because of it. If I could trust my body more, let it go more, I often think, I might do better.

I took middle-stump guard, as I do every innings. Against fast bowlers I'm fairly well across towards the off stump, with my bat on centre, by my right toe. I make a mark with the inside spike of my right foot, a mark I will consult through the innings, and stand with my feet up to that mark. What is important to me is to know where my off stump is because anything outside that I aim to let go at the start of an innings. The Australians basically bowl off-stump or just outside to get you caught in the slips or at the wicket. They don't worry about wasting balls as much as we do because they are trying to get that precise distance outside off-stump so that you don't know whether or not to play the ball.

I then looked round the field. Thomson, whom I didn't face until the last five balls of the evening, had brought up everybody except fine leg. He always has five or six slip fielders but this time, for the last short burst, he even brought cover point into silly mid-off. He couldn't have got more attacking but this didn't bother me. With that attacking field, if he did pitch it up, which he would have to do every now and again, I knew if I came into the ball firmly there would be some ones and twos to be had to mid-off or cover or mid-on.

I looked especially for the short leg because for a certain ball, one about middle-and-leg that bounces high, there is a danger of being caught at short leg. It is important to know that if the short leg is just in front of square, you can get out of trouble at the last moment by turning the ball behind square, which I had just done against Max Walker.

I then tick off a few check-points of my stance, though rather less meticulously than some golfers such as Jack Nicklaus or, I'm told, Graham Marsh, whose brother, incidentally, was a full sixty feet behind me at the time. Is my head upright? 'Keep your head still.' Are my hands holding the bat easily?

I hum to ease the tension. I like to let musical themes run through my head and my favourite is a cello passage from the Rasoumoffsky Quartets. I use the music like a talisman: how can I ever be out with this tune running through my head? I was comfortable. It was cool that evening and my helmet wasn't sweaty and my chest-protector, a pad nine inches square, felt snug. (Boycott, Knott and I wear chest protectors occasionally.)

Thomson reached his mark. He glared. I stopped humming. I replaced it with a different theme – 'take it easy, you'll see him soon enough' – and he started in. I have never seen him come in from such a long run-up, about fifty yards. I don't like to concentrate on a fast bowler until he is well into his run-up, perhaps half-way, because you get over-impressed by his power and speed and become mesmerised. As he approaches the wicket, I stand up and lift my bat high.

Thomson's unusual catapult-like action makes it sometimes hard to pick up the ball early. At Old Trafford the screens are better than on any other Test ground, and I cannot remember having difficulty seeing the ball. As he delivers the ball, I move a little onto the back foot. This movement gives me a fraction of a second longer to react, and it does not prevent me from coming forward into the ball if it is pitched up.

One thing that gives me pleasure is playing a fast bowler straight back down the pitch. Thomson bowled one to me that was just slightly leg-side, fairly well up, and I played it perfectly balanced, coming into the ball and it went to mid-on for two. I hit another ball to cover for two. When play ended that day I had six runs on the board. I was satisfied.

Cutting Norman Gifford for 4 during my highest innings of the season, 152, at Lord's. Middlesex won by an innings and 10 runs. Worcester wicket-keeper is D. J. Humphries. Photograph by courtesy of Sport and General

I love batting. My own experience is that it is extremely hard to link external events in my life with success or failure on the field. One of the beautiful things about cricket, which it shares with the arts, is that life becomes simplified in the absorption of bowling, wicket-keeping and, especially, batting. The job is difficult but the task relatively straightforward. Broken marriages, conflicts of loyalty, the problems of everyday life fall away as one faces up to Thomson.

I needed many years as a professional cricketer before I became happy with a technique and aware of my strengths and limitations. One-day cricket has meant that in general it takes longer for batsmen to develop to Test standard. My technique also changed as a result of remarks from colleagues and coaches. A striking improvement came after an innings at Birmingham on 8 May 1974. I scored a painful 78 before Willis had me caught behind. 'Tiger' Smith, then 87 years old, Warwickshire's ex-wicket-keeper and ex-coach, gave me his stick and told me to hold it like a bat. He pointed out that I was gripping it far too tightly, and that my face was frowning and tense. He asked me to relax. He also suggested that I stood up higher just before the ball was bowled, partly as a rhythm for relaxation, partly to prevent me falling over towards the off side. Tiger said: 'Now you can bring your left hand straight down to the line of ball.' I always have a chat with Tiger when I play at Edgbaston.

John Hughes produced this table of my career. What interests me most is the clarity with which these figures show how I marked time as a batsman between 1964 and 1973. Apart from the freakish tour of Pakistan in 1967, my average over this period was consistently modest, ranging from 23 to 31. The 1973 season was the turning point. I went in number 3 all season and scored my first championship century. Half-way through 1974 I started opening again.

The next morning Amiss and I continued. The conventional way of calling

BREARLEY, J. M.

SEASON	COUNTRY	M.	I.	N.O.	RUNS	H.S.	AVER.	100	50	0	RUNS	WKTS.	AVER.	CT.	ST.
1961	Eng.	21	40	6	1222	145*	35·94	2	8	—	—	—	—	47	3
1962	Eng.	17	33	4	950	113*	32·75	2	4	4	4	0	∝	24	6
1963	Eng.	16	28	2	790	100	30·38	1	4	1	27	1	27·00	18	1
1964	Eng.	29	54	5	2178	169	44·44	5	11	5	31	0	∝	23	—
1964–65	S. Africa	12	19	3	406	68	25·37	—	2	3	—	—	—	12	—
1965	Eng.	29	50	6	1024	90*	23·27	—	5	6	13	0	∝	15	—
1966	Eng.	2	4	0	114	101	28·50	1	—	1	7	0	∝	1	—
1967	Pak.	6	9	3	793	312*	132·16	2	3	—	9	0	∝	12	—
1968	Eng.	18	32	3	736	91	25·37	—	4	2	—	—	—	13	2
1969	Eng.	7	10	0	253	75	25·30	—	2	—	—	—	—	5	—
1970	Eng.	10	17	1	471	85	29·43	—	4	3	—	—	—	4	—
1971	Eng.	22	35	4	979	81*	31·58	—	9	4	—	—	—	19	—
1972	Eng.	22	37	8	877	75	30·24	—	4	3	—	—	—	22	—
1973	Eng.	20	32	4	1095	134*	39·10	1	9	2	—	—	—	11	—
1973–74	Pak.	2	4	0	220	115	55·00	1	1	—	10	0	∝	—	—
1973–74	E. Africa	1	2	0	45	26	22·50	—	—	—	—	—	—	2	—
1974	Eng.	21	36	5	1324	173*	42·70	2	7	3	—	—	—	20	—
1975	Eng.	20	39	8	1656	150	53·41	4	10	1	4	0	∝	14	—
1976	Eng.	25	45	3	1695	153	40·35	4	7	1	0	0	∝	15	—
1976–77	India	12	16	1	714	202	47·60	1	6	—	—	—	—	12	—
1976–77	Aust.	2	4	1	174	61	58·00	—	2	—	—	—	—	1	—
1977	Eng.	20	31	4	1251	152	46·33	3	5	3	—	—	—	15	—
TOTAL		334	577	71	18967	312*	37·48	29	107	42	105	1	105·00	305	12

City of London School XI 1956–60 1959: runs 1015; av. 84. 1960: runs 615; av. 68.

prescribes that the striker calls Yes, No, or Wait for virtually all the shots he plays in front of the wicket or just behind square. Dennis prefers to leave more to the non-striker; he likes to push the ball and look for a run, inviting his partner to send him back. I am aware of this when I bat with him. He was struggling but he stuck it out.

That morning I faced O'Keeffe and Bright, too. What I say to myself against slow bowlers is 'don't move too soon, wait before you commit yourself forward or back'. In that innings I don't think I played-and-missed at all. I didn't edge the ball once. Thomson was bowling very well but I think I only once got into difficulty with him: it was a ball just short of a length, middle-stump and it 'got big', hit my glove and went down to gulley; it could easily have gone up.

Defence, when it is coming smoothly and naturally, offers great satisfaction. One of the most difficult things to do is to judge which ball to let go, especially the fast balls, since there is a tendency to stab involuntarily at a ball just outside off-stump. It requires confidence to stand very still and let the ball go by, just evading it when it bounces high, without having any risk of being hit or getting a glove or an edge of a bat on the ball.

The critics and textbooks say that you should always get behind the ball against fast bowling. When I was in Perth in the spring of 1977 and got about 60 in each innings against Lillee, Malone, and another quick bowler, Clark, I realized that if you got behind a ball at about off-stump, just short of a length, that bounced chest-high, there was precious little you could do about it. Either you got hit in the chest or on the gloves. One answer, I learned, is to sway back inside the ball.

One of the Western Australia players, Ian Brayshaw, helped me by saying that when Dennis Lillee bowls at Perth, which is a notoriously bouncy wicket, he reckons that 95 per cent of the balls would not hit the stumps. They would go over the top or just outside the off or the leg stump. Letting Lillee's balls go by gave me confidence and, although English wickets aren't the same, this method has helped me deal with short-pitched bowling.

I began to get on top of Thomson. I remember two fours. Having got used to the bounce of the pitch I set myself to cut. Intentionally, I played his next short ball high over the slips. The next ball was further up and I stood up and steered it between gulley and slip in a controlled way for the other four.

There is obviously a sensual satisfaction in hitting a ball sweetly, in the middle of a good bat, exactly where you meant to hit it, especially an attacking shot. There is a pleasure in playing each ball on its merits, exactly right, feeling you're moving perfectly to the ball. The sensual satisfactions also take their place in the longer arc of the whole innings.

But then I got out. Amiss had scored a single, and I was facing O'Keeffe. I tried to drive: the ball stopped a little, and I hit it straight to Walters. It was on my mind that we only needed four runs to win and I was tempted by the idea that it would be nice to win the match with one shot: a silly, childish thought.

8 The Return of the Prodigal

The Third Test

Brearley arrived at Trent Bridge, Nottingham, on the day before the Third Test. It was here at Nottingham a summer before, that he played his first match for England. That was against the West Indies, a series in which he played two matches, and he remembered the game with mixed feelings: in the first innings, knees shaking, he was caught for a duck at fourth slip by Viv Richards off his fourth ball from Bernard Julien; in the second innings, again taking the new ball, he had played for 50 minutes before being caught at wicket for 17 by Deryck Murray off a ball from Vanburn Holder.

The most important decision taken over the Third Test was made at Lord's six days before the match. The selectors decided, unanimously, to pick Geoff Boycott to play once again for England. Achilles, who had been skulking in his tent for years, could not have been more warmly welcomed back into the Grecian ranks. The Prodigal Son returned.

He had made himself available for the Second Test. I had been inclined to pick him then, though I could appreciate the reluctance of some selectors; they felt they did not want to come just when he whistled, or change a team that had been doing well for one individual.

I think the whole selection was sound. Boycott, Hendrick and Roope were brought in for Amiss, Lever and Barlow. Old was unfit, and was replaced by Botham.

There is an old chestnut that you should never change a winning side. As a blanket argument, I think this is fatuous. If you have the chance to strengthen a side, you do so whether or not it won the last match. Conversely, you should resist pressures to change a losing side just because it lost.

It was sad, though, to leave out my tour colleagues. Most captains find the business of dropping players the most unwelcome aspect of their job. Amiss is a tremendously courageous and consistent player; Lever seemed a bit jaded after his hard winter, and poor Barlow was totally out of form.

But I was excited about the new side. Mike Hendrick had been working at his own hard training schedule, as had all the Derbyshire players now that Eddie Barlow was in charge. He was running 3 miles against the clock, doing 50 press-ups and other exercises every day. This season he was bowling better than ever. He moves the ball either way, very late. His height and accuracy make it desperately hard for the batsman to drive him. Graham Roope, too, was having a

Boycott at
Nottingham. The cap
is back where it
belongs

good year; Fred Titmus told me at the Oval that Roope was playing sensibly
and maturely. He is also one of the best close fielders in England. Boycott, of
course, is unquestionably the best and most experienced batsman in England.

The only change that was forced on us was the filling of the gap left by Old.
We had no hesitation about bringing in Ian Botham. His progress since he was
on the Lord's ground staff three years ago has been fantastic. As a batsman, he is
aggressive and brave. Botham is in the Australian mould as a cricketer: strong,
assertive, likeable, straightforward, a bit raw.

The selectors are rather like Modern Parents – taken for granted except when
things go wrong. They also contribute to what goes right. The meetings took

The selectors at Trent Bridge, 10 o'clock, first morning.

Left to right: Brearley, Ken Barrington, John Murray, Charles Elliott with his cigar (a smaller one than usual), Alec Bedser. We were deciding, then, that of the twelve Roope should be left out. It was not an easy choice; we thought the pitch would be a bit more bouncy than it was; we didn't think it would turn much (correct), but we thought that Miller might play Pascoe and Thomson as well as Roope. He played Lillee and Malone exceptionally well at Perth. Also, Miller had done a useful job in the Second Test, so that it would have been hard on him to be left out. A nice study in concentration, and a pleasant reminder for me of the many hours we spent together. The selectors become virtually members of the side, and a successful year is as gratifying to them as it is to the players.

place on Friday evenings, in a small room at Lord's. The starting time often depended on what time my match finished.

This meeting began late, as Middlesex's important match with Gloucestershire did not end until 6.20 p.m. It was an amazing and for us frustrating match. Gloucestershire followed on 263 behind, on a bad wicket, then scored 337. We needed 75 to win and were allowed 12 overs (we thought it should have been 13). We finished with 63 for 7. Another result of this match was that during my innings of 145, Mike Procter had hit me two or three times on the left knee, which next day was swollen. Medical advice was that I should not risk aggravation by playing over the weekend.

At the meeting, the knee was exhibit A, and one of the selectors' topics which continued after I left was who would replace me in the unlikely event of my not being fit for the Test.

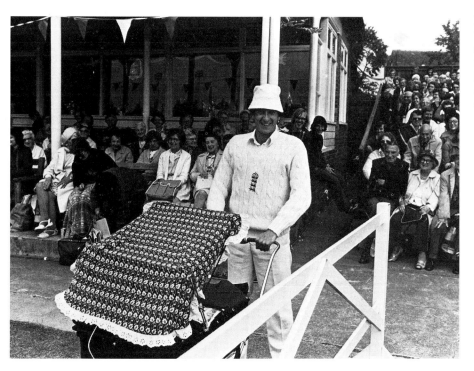

Big Daddy Randall at Trent Bridge, and all smiles in the Ladies' Stand. The baby (Simon) was born in early May 'He's champion,' Derek says

Charlie Elliott and I usually drink red wine, the others started with a beer. After an hour or so, we helped ourselves to the salads and cheese that were left ready for us. The Chairman was often the one who said 'Come on now, we've got to settle this, you know.' Often most difficult questions arose not over the main selection, but over the question of cover for each player; we tried to decide on a replacement for everyone, in case of injury or illness. This often led to complicated hypotheticals, like 'What happens if Knott is injured, *and* the bowler unfit is Botham, will the batting be too weak if Lever comes in for Botham and Taylor for Knott?'

When the team has been chosen, cards and instructions are sent to each player. These arrive on Monday morning. It seems to me an unnecessarily cruel way of discovering you have been dropped to hear the side on the radio at Sunday lunchtime. In 1976 when I arrived at Bath for the Sunday League game the old dressing room attendant said to me 'Them've dropped that fellow of your'n, what they do call 'ee, that Brearley'; they hadn't, actually, but they did next match, and then I heard it second-hand from a radio announcement. So I told Lever and Barlow at Lord's next day when we played Essex, and phoned Amiss who was staying at Tony Greig's. Inclusions are not so difficult to take. Boycott and the others learned of theirs from the radio.

The gates at Trent Bridge were closed soon after the start, on each of the first four days. I have never known such scenes of enthusiasm and support. Going down to breakfast in the hotel overlooking the ground at 9 o'clock, we would

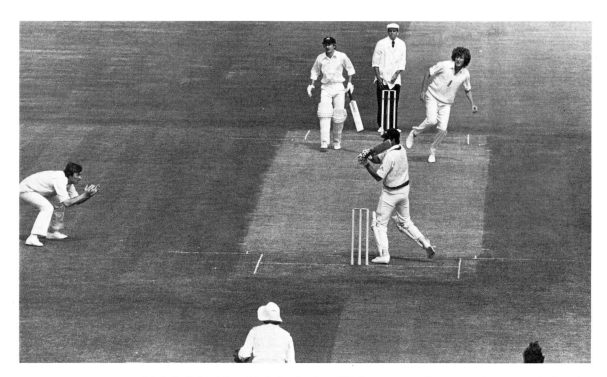

5th ball of Third Test. McCosker hooks Willis for 4. Non-striker Ian Davis. We soon had to give up our idea of attacking McCosker with the bouncer on this pitch. In the slips we had already moved two or three yards closer to the bat, having expected the pitch to be bouncier on the first morning. At Melbourne, Willis had broken McCosker's jaw. In the first two Tests, he had scored few runs and had fallen to Willis three times, the last time – at Old Trafford – mishooking a bouncer in the first over of the innings. Yet here he played courageously and superbly to make 51 and 107 in the match. We started with Woolmer in at short square-leg in case McCosker after his recent unhappy experiences did not go for the hook shot, but here he had plenty of time for the shot. He has got well inside the line and has rolled his wrists nicely. Several times Willis did not quite bowl at his best during the first few overs of the Tests, a combination of tension and of bowling at McCosker, who scores so freely if the line strays at all towards leg-stump. He, Willis, does not look as though he is following through as energetically as he would have done a few overs later. Davis too played well this morning, until he presented us with his wicket.

see already perhaps five thousand in the ground, filling the best seats in the pavilion, booking favoured patches of grass at the boundary edge. As we walked into the pavilion one by one we were greeted with little bursts of applause, Randall and Boycott by big bursts. Net practices were watched by thousands of fans. And for most of the match, until the ominously thundery last day, the weather was sunny and warm but not too hot.

At the start of the match the papers carried the story that Thomson was withdrawing from Packer's matches since he already had a contract which depended on his playing for Queensland and Australia. When he came in to bat, he was clapped all the way to the crease. Conversely, Greig had a mixed reception of cheers and boos when he came in, especially in the second innings;

Melbourne, 2nd innings. McCosker hooks Lever. This was three days after he had broken his jaw, and he was still almost unrecognizable. At the time I thought he ought not to have batted, certainly not at No. 10 (rather than No. 11), because it was hard for us to bowl flat-out at him. However, perhaps he laid the ghost quicker this way. Also, surprisingly, without his stand of 54 with Marsh, Australia may well have lost the match

but I think the crowd may partly have been expressing its disappointment that he was in front of Randall in the batting order. On the whole, it was a marvellous crowd, generous and enthusiastic.

My Jubilee crown came down tails again, and Chappell chose to bat. Pascoe was back in for Bright; Roope was our twelfth man.

The morning belonged to Australia, the afternoon, much more dramatically, to England. In 2 hours, 7 wickets fell for only 65 runs. At lunch, there was not the slightest indication of what was to come. The pitch was excellent, the outfield fast, the light good. Tony used to give a little up-and-at-'em talk each

McCosker c. Brearley b. Hendrick 51. Trent Bridge, first day. The ball only just carried. We were standing in an uncomfortable little dip there, which made it hard to know how far the ball would carry. My hands are nicely positioned for the catch, fingers down. We were standing as close as we could, since there was not that much bounce in the pitch. It was a good length ball, fractionally outside the off stump, which moved away a little. McCosker followed it, and edged it.

The picture shows how still Knott and Greig have stayed. At first slip I stand a little deeper than both of them, and it's important for me not to get distracted by unnecessary movements towards the ball.

The Australians have a different method. Their first slip stands almost as close as the wicket-keeper, and almost level with second slip. We prefer the more staggered arrangement mainly so that there's less risk of each slip leaving the ball to the man next to him. If you're staggered, both can go for the ball without risk of collision.

Notice how far and how straight Hendrick follows through. Most of the footmarks visible at this end were his. He bowls from quite close to the stumps, and doesn't fall away. Geoff Miller said to me that when Hendrick has bowled the first over for Derbyshire, you can't see a mark on the ball since every delivery has pitched on the seam. He bowls with everything straight, run-up straight, arm straight, hand upright, behind the ball, follow-through straight – all this gives him the best chance of landing the ball on the seam.

time we left the dressing-room to field; I did this less, but on this occasion I remember saying, 'Look, this is where we may be really tested. I want everyone going just as hard if they're 230 for 1 as when we're right on top.'

Hendrick bowled excellently for an hour from the pavilion end. He had McCosker caught at slip by me, and frustrated Chappell by his perfect length and line. After drinks, I put Botham on in his place. Earlier, he had nearly taken a wicket with his second ball in Test cricket (I had not given him a third slip). But then he strayed towards leg-stump and McCosker scored five more 4s off him in as many overs, all on the leg side. Now, from the opposite end, he bowled to Chappell. His first ball was fairly innocuous, but Chappell tried to force off the back foot and edged it into his stumps. Hendrick caught Hookes, brilliantly, at slip and Botham had Walters caught by the same fielder. In came Marsh. Botham had bowled well in the MCC *v* Australians match, occasionally surprising them with his quicker ball. His one bad patch came against Marsh, after he hooked a bouncer for four. Ian felt he had to retaliate, with the result that he was hooked and cut for another 20 runs in less than two overs before I took him off.

Trent Bridge. Robinson c. Brearley b. Greig. Hendrick 2nd slip. One of the many slip catches held by us in this match. Photograph by courtesy of Central Press Photos

The Queen's visit to Nottingham. Australians (left to right): Robinson, Bright, Cosier, Hookes, Davis, Chappell. England: Woolmer, Willis, Roope, Brearley, Botham. Photograph by courtesy of Central Press Photos

Had he learned the lesson of this little duel? I had certainly rubbed it in before the game: never bowl a bouncer out of machismo, to prove a point; unless you're Lillee's pace, only bowl them occasionally, for a specific purpose, to surprise rather than to intimidate.

Botham bowled superbly. He did try one bouncer, which surprised Marsh, who was late on his shot. Soon, Ian swung one in and had him plumb l.b.w.

By the end of the innings he had also dismissed Walker and Thomson to finish with 5 for 74. He got his wickets by concentrating mainly on his out-swinger, bowled to a full length at or outside the off stump.

The Queen and Prince Philip were presented to the teams after tea. They had been at Mansfield when all the wickets fell.

Once again we had to survive for half an hour or so. I said I would take first ball. Geoff Boycott was, naturally, nervous. We had not batted together for twelve years, since the MCC tour of South Africa.

Next day the first half belonged to Australia, the second half, more dramatically, to England. The whole day belonged to Boycott. Pascoe and

Thomson bowled with fire, but rarely beat his bat. It was an epic struggle. In 3 hours, he scored only 20. We slid from 34 for 0 to 82 for 5. Then Pascoe forced Boycott to play at a good length ball that left him; it found the edge, and went knee-high to McCosker, who missed the catch. From that point on, our fortunes revived.

Alan Knott's innings had started in character. He played back, turned to face the bowler, and held his bat up in front of his body like a French-cricket player. Anything wide he left severely alone. Against quick bowlers, he always holds the bat with his left hand behind the handle – quite unlike his normal grip. He can play higher this way.

Knott applies thought to his own technique as thoroughly as anyone I know. He does not waste energy. When he watches, he looks very closely and with questions in mind, like a scholar reading a book. When he has a net, it is almost always to practise something specific, like playing high, or letting the ball go, or sweeping.

Almost imperceptibly, he started to attack. He chipped the ball away on the

Poor McCosker. 1st innings at Trent Bridge, England 87 for 5, Boycott 20. Doug Walters at 3rd slip. A fairly straightforward chance off Pascoe. Geoff's right hand has come off the bat, which suggests that he might have been taking his bat away at the last minute

Knott at Nottingham. It's not clear from this picture whether Knott has steered this ball down, or sliced it over the slips. This latter shot he plays intentionally against fast bowling on bouncy pitches. He did it in Australia in 1974–5 when he scored his first Test century. It's a shot that is liable to irritate any fast bowler, and is relatively easy to play once you have gauged the pace of the pitch. Alan looks for the short ball, and aims to stay inside the line, if necessary moving back slightly towards square-leg. Then, as it goes by, he steers it with minimal movement high over the slips. A slight variation of this shot is what we use for slip practice. Though it has served him well over the years, Knott was out twice in the series – at Manchester and Nottingham – caught at third man. Definitely *not* a shot from the MCC coaching book, but a useful variation for an advanced student!

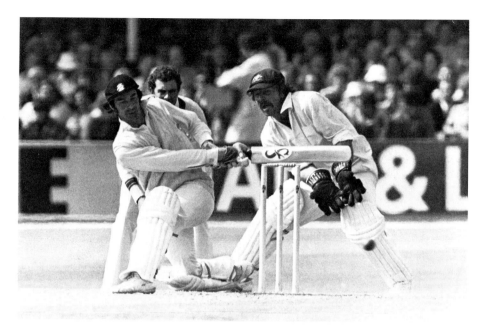

Knott sweeping O'Keeffe. Judging by Marsh's hands, I'd guess that the ball was just missing leg-stump, but it may have been straight. It looks as if Marsh has first tried to get a glimpse of the ball to the offside of Knott, so his head is there, while his hands move towards leg with the ball as it dipped in. (O'Keeffe's leg-spin action often makes the ball drift in from the off.) Knott, like Compton, sets himself to sweep on the length rather than the line. He concentrates on keeping his head still, getting low, putting his front leg between the ball and the stumps. He thinks one great fault in most batsmen when they play this shot is that they try to hit the ball too hard. He does little more than help the ball towards square- or long-leg. The main risk is the top edge; Knott rarely gets out this way, I imagine, because he has such a wonderful eye. He had fascinating duels in India with Bishen Bedi: Bedi would often put his short leg either about three yards deeper than usual behind square, or back saving one. A lot of nonsense is talked about the sweep shot – I remember Jim Swanton referring to it as 'that infernal stroke'. With Alan Knott, it is an exquisite stroke, one that, together with all his others, make it sometimes impossible to bowl spinners to this inventive impish batsman.

Knott sweeps O'Keeffe at Old Trafford. This one is a foot wide of the off stump at least. Even Knott looks as if he's gone a bit far this time! What to bowl next?

Above:

Randall run out at Trent Bridge. What happened was this: Geoffrey pushed a ball from Thomson firmly back down the wicket between the stumps and the non-striker. He said 'Wait', then thinking the ball had gone past Thomson, 'Yes'. Thomson, who falls away after bowling, recovered extraordinarily quickly, and darted back towards the ball. Randall had hesitated, understandably. He could have prevented the run-out if at this point he had shouted 'No'. Thomson fumbled the ball but still had plenty of time to flick it into Marsh, who demolished the stumps. In the picture Robinson, who has come from short leg, is in front of Randall, then, left to right, Thomson, Marsh, Boycott, Chappell, Pascoe, O'Keeffe, McCosker. Umpire Bird has gone racing off out of the picture to look for a possible run-out at the bowler's end.

Boycott's running and calling have, in the past, been suspect. This incident was doubly unfortunate in that he has improved enormously. I found him excellent in this respect. He insists that both batsmen concentrate fully *all* the time, especially when not facing the bowling. It is up to the non-striker to make sure his partner knows if any fielders out of his view change their position; he can also avert trouble by a quick loud 'No'. Few fast bowlers are as athletic or mobile as Thomson, whom Boycott had faced very little before this Test match.

leg side, and started to cut the short-pitched ball. Quite suddenly, the balance had shifted, as if we had finished one film and started another. Boycott hit Pascoe square on the off side for his first boundary. Knott drove Walker through extra cover for four. When O'Keeffe came on, he swept him; then cut him delicately, from off-stump, for two hours in an over. Boycott grew in confidence and control. He was uneasy at the liberties Knott took with O'Keeffe, and suggested to him that he played O'Keeffe more carefully. Next day they reached their hundreds almost at the same time. Their stand of 215 was the highest of the series and, I think, the best.

Geoffrey's performance was remarkable. Pascoe in particular and Thomson had bowled very fast and well. Pascoe was warned by Umpire Bird for bowling four bouncers in an over against Boycott early on. He rarely got into difficulty against the short ball. Once or twice he was hit on the glove, and once or twice he took a blow on his chest-guard. When the ball bounced above chest height, he evaded it well, never taking his eye off it. His judgement of what to leave outside the off stump was unerring. He became increasingly confident about where short singles were to be had, after the disastrous mix-up with Randall.

In the intervals, he would move quietly about the dressing-room, thinking and sometimes talking about the situation. He is meticulous about his gear, having everything laid out ready. He checks it all thoroughly before the match. As he says, he doesn't want to be able to blame anything outside himself for mistakes he may make. The story is told that long ago he snapped back at someone who wished him luck as he went out to bat, 'It's not luck, it's skill.' He is a perfectionist.

When we batted together at the Oval in the Fifth Test, Boycott for once played-and-missed more often than I did. But he was concerned to say that he didn't play-and-miss 'properly' more than four or five times. Oddly enough, John Arlott in his book on the 1953 Series comments that it was not always easy to tell whether Len Hutton took his bat out of the way or played at the ball. Geoffrey wants both to eliminate mistakes and to be seen and assessed fairly.

Perfectionism can of course emerge as obsession with safety, simple avoidance of risk. If you never drive a car at more than 10 m.p.h. you do not get very far, and you can contribute to others taking too many chances. But without perfectionism where is the drive to improve? Like Boycott, I too am kept going by the lure of the ideal.

In this match Pascoe showed himself a bowler who could become a worthy successor to Lillee. On this excellent pitch he found more life than Willis or Thomson. When the crucial catch was dropped, off him, he had bowled 19 overs and taken three wickets for 20. On the field he has a slightly fanatical air, with his aggressive glare and his Trueman-like black hair. Early in the tour we nicknamed him 'The Separatist', referring to his Yugoslavian origins. Off the field he is quiet-spoken and mild; I preferred to see him in this vein.

Lenny Pascoe at Trent Bridge. He bowled magnificently in this match. For the first time he was very fast without losing control. He extracted more life from this pitch than Willis or Thomson, and deserved better figures than 4 for 123. At one stage he had 3 for 20 off 19 overs.

Left:
Dicky Bird looks tense

Right:
Pascoe leans away and opens up slightly more than the text-book might suggest

At the end of the third day, Australia were 112 for 2, 7 runs behind. Hendrick had taken the vital wicket. I thought Chappell showed less willingness to fight it out than before. McCosker though, was still there. We had to bowl them out in a day.

Knott afterwards described the fourth day as the most tense day of Test cricket that he could remember. Every wicket was crucial. Each time we felt the game was slipping away, we would prise someone out. It was a fantastic achievement of bowling and fielding to dismiss Australia twice in those conditions. Willis came back time after time to bowl as Greig had asked in Sydney. Hendrick and Underwood gave nothing at all away; Underwood got another victim from over the wicket. Botham and Greig both bowled well.

I received criticism and even some vitriolic letters demanding to know why I did not bowl Miller more, in both the Second and Third Tests. I think I was right to use him sparingly. In each match, the game was tight. Underwood is the most reliable spinner in the world, and I would almost always want to try him first, as there is no risk of the pressure being let off. We rarely wanted two spinners on at once, since the quicker bowlers nearly always looked dangerous. The ball swung a little most days of the series. At Old Trafford, two of Geoff's victims were left-handers playing at balls that pitched in the rough; the third succumbed to a full-toss. I have a lot of time for Miller. He has become meaner as

Chappell b. Hendrick 27. Second innings, Nottingham. Umpire: D. Constant; non-striker: McCosker. Chappell looked slightly reckless at the start of this innings. He got off the mark against Willis with an off-drive for 4 that went in the air very close to Randall. He reached 20 in no time, but with several loose shots. Australia had a deficit of 120 on the first innings; it was as if he could not raise the mental effort required to graft it out if necessary. At tea, we felt we could get him out and that Hendrick was the man for the job. In the first innings he had bowled accurately at Chappell for an hour; when Botham replaced him Chappell had played casually at his first ball and was bowled.

This ball was of good length, pitching just outside the off stump. Chappell went back, trying to force, and was bowled off the inside edge. He is somewhat square-on, probably from the adjustment he made when the ball came in from the off

a bowler without losing flight or spin; as a batsman he has everything except the invaluable experience of some centuries behind him.

The fourth day ended with yet another half hour session for us. We needed 189 to win. That night I had dinner with John Arlott and Tony Lewis. John said, 'The great thing about you, Mike, is that you're the only England captain who knows it doesn't *really* matter.' But we were all three buoyant and excited about the next day's prospects.

Walters driving Greig, 2nd innings. This was exactly like the shot which Walters got out to this innings, caught at cover off Greig. The bat flows beautifully out in the direction of the shot, the head is still. The left leg is straighter and the right side more forward than would be approved of by the English purist. Australians however have always used more bottom hand for their cover-drive. Walters plays the shot superbly. Hendrick and me at slip

Dicky Bird happened to be there, so we invited him over for a drink after our meal. He is a nervous, amusing and delightful man. I not only respect his umpiring, I also enjoy his company during a match. Umpires are supposed to be calming influences on the players from time to time; I sometimes take that role with him: 'Come on Dicky, relax; it's only a game.' My only complaint with him is that he requires a degree of certainty that is almost neurotic, like that of a man who has to keep going back to the front door to make certain he's locked it. That evening I said to him, half joking, 'Dicky, there is no such thing as absolute certainty, only the certainty that befits the subject. What is certain or accurate for a carpenter is not certain or accurate for a geometer.' I did not spell out in too much detail the relevance of Aristotle's point to l.b.w. decisions; I was batting the next day, and I did not want him suddenly to adopt less exacting standards of certainty.

One feature of this Trent Bridge match was the excellence of the umpiring. Bird and David Constant are probably the best umpires in the country. One decision by Constant was, I thought, outstanding. In the Australian's second innings, Robinson came down late on a ball from Underwood. It hit his pad first, then the bat. Constant gave him out l.b.w. Most umpires are reluctant to give a man out when the ball only brushes the pad and then hits the middle of the bat.

Oddly enough, one mistake went unnoticed by almost everyone, certainly by all the players. On Saturday morning, after the drinks interval Boycott and Knott went back to the wrong ends. The first I heard of this was from Irving Rosenwater in October. He had checked with both scorers.

Cover-drive. Leaning
back slightly too
much

I slept well, as usual. I have never had to take sleeping pills during Tests, as
several do. Next day, again, the peculiar tension of slow, absorbing cricket
continued. Only in Test cricket, with its risk of boredom, does one also have the
time and the rhythm for such long-drawn out climaxes – Sunday afternoons
produce cheap thrills compared with the Trent Bridge Test of 1977.

The end of the catapult. Thomson bowling to me at Nottingham. His right arm has gone from by his right calf through 400°. Boycott and Pascoe in the picture. Geoffrey is letting his gloves and hands dry

Right:
Drinks at Trent Bridge. Thunderstorm at Sleaford! I usually drink water, squash if I haven't remembered to ask for any. Also provided are salt tablets, glucose, and chewing gum

As it turned out, it was not only psychological electricity that was in the air. Boycott and I had seen us to the half-way point at lunch, the match seemed almost won, when Alec Bedser came in with the news that the local Meteorological Office report just received said that there was a risk of heavy thunderstorms in the Nottingham area from 4 o'clock on. We decided we should try to win the match by tea, i.e. score 95 runs in two hours.

In the first hour after lunch I played with more freedom, even panache, than usual. Geoffrey gave me the strike, and we were ahead of our target. Phil Slocombe had later news with the drinks: 'heavy rain over Sleaford, storm centre approaching'. I gave instructions that Knott, Greig and Randall should come in at 3, 4 and 5. It would be insufferable if the rain came with us 20 runs short.

In the event, after I was out, both Knott and Greig fell in 5 minutes, so I said to Randall, 'You'd better take it easy for a while; but keep an eye on the sky, both of you.' In the event it did not rain, but a friend told me that he came through torrential rain driving through Newark, 20 miles away, at 4 o'clock. We won shortly after tea, by seven wickets.

There were many outstanding performances. Botham's, Knott's and Willis' for us, Pascoe's and McCosker's for Australia. But of course the hero was Boycott, who batted on every one of the five days. His was an eloquent answer to the critics who had questioned his ability, and to those who secretly or otherwise would not have minded him failing.

Knott, Underwood, Brearley and Greig during the Third Test at Trent Bridge

The Oval, second day, after first day washed out. Those storm clouds looked dangerously close to Lord's, where Middlesex were racing home in the Gillette semi-final against Somerset, the match that we had tried to play on five different days. Boycott is taking guard, about to face Malone's first over. Thomson has just completed his first over from this end

9 Yorkshire and England

The Fourth Test

A fortnight after the season ended I was on holiday in Switzerland, sitting on a park bench in Basle, dictating my impressions of the Headingley match on a tape recorder. I thought of the incident to open the chapter. 'Chappell is bowling from the grandstand end, to Boycott, the ball swings very slightly away, well up, almost a half-volley, and he's driven it straight back at the non-striking batsman for four and it's his hundredth 100. He's done it at Headingley, in a Test match against Australia. It was a beautiful shot, perfectly controlled, he let the ball come, bent his knee, picked his spot and almost hit Graham Roope. The achievement of the match.'

Looking at the roofs of the old city and the brown Rhine, imagining Boycott's shot, I remembered the Yorkshire youngsters, and some older than youngsters, sweeping onto the field and briefly stealing his cap. It indeed was the achievement of the match, but the achievement of the season, in terms of England, was finally fulfilled three days later when we captured the Ashes. In fact, Boycott's century fell within the span of some of the most enthralling cricketing days, on and off the Test pitch, of the summer of 1977. Geoff himself began it the previous Saturday at Edgbaston when, in the County match against Warwickshire, he set out towards his ninety-ninth first-class 100 which he achieved by Monday.

On the same Saturday, Middlesex were due to start the three-day Championship match at Lord's. We met during Saturday's rain and requested to see Jack Bannister, Secretary of the Cricketers' Association. The majority of our players were against the Test and County Cricket Board's threat to suspend players who affiliated with Kerry Packer, and expressed worry over the possible costs of the impending court case. We questioned the right of our officials to speak on our behalf without an extraordinary meeting of the Association. We also asked that some effort be made for our representatives to meet Packer.

We had had no play at all on the Saturday, and only 23 minutes on Monday, when Surrey scored 8 for 1 wicket. On Tuesday morning, the pitch looked green and damp: good conditions for Mike Selvey who reckoned we would bowl Surrey out twice in the day and win. We did exactly that, despite dropping five catches. We wanted to forfeit our first innings altogether, to save time, but a rarely cited law of the game states that this can only be done in a side's second innings, so we had to receive one ball before declaring at 0 for 0. In

Opposite, top: Fourth Test: Chappell c. Brearley b. Hendrick

Opposite, below: Part of Malone's marathon at the Oval. Well-stained shirt. Non-striker: Lever. Umpire: Spencer

The hundredth-100 run. A perfect shot, too. Marsh's position and the position of Boycott's left foot indicate that the ball was outside the off stump. Half-volley, swinging away slightly: instead of hitting it to mid-off he picked his spot and drove it back at the non-striker

the end, we needed 139 to win in 27 minutes plus 20 overs. We completed a dramatic day by winning by nine wickets with 11 balls to spare. (Mike Smith scored 51 and I got 66 not out.) We moved back ahead of Kent to first place in the Championship.

I also met potential agents. I had been approached with the argument that at my age I would be foolish not to try to use my belated success financially. I accepted the argument; but I did not feel entirely easy about it. The Puritan streak in my character said that I should not set out to earn money from activities that I would not do for their own sake. Years ago I felt a similar qualm about revelling in success on the field, as if the pleasure *ought* to be more inward, more intrinsic to the performance. Now I have reached a healthier attitude to success and failure, somewhere between obsession and pretended unconcern. I know I want to do well; I also know that success does not fill emotional voids for long.

When I arrived at Headingley the day after we beat Surrey, Derek Underwood said, 'You deserve to win the Championship title if you bowl a side out twice in a day.'

At the team dinner that evening Alec Bedser congratulated us all and Geoff Boycott in particular for the performance in the Third Test at Trent Bridge. Brian Rose had been added to the twelve in case Bob Woolmer's bruised hand did not improve sufficiently. After we had all had our say on tactics, Brian said that he had been in Australia the previous winter, and he would like nothing more than that we should really rub their noses in it. I think that many Englishmen agreed that it was time that we became good winners and the Australians good losers.

We discussed too David Evans' initiative. Evans, a company chairman and keen ex-cricketer, had found three businessmen willing to give £9,000 to the players. They had initially wanted it to go only to the nine players who were not involved with Packer. I had had several telephone conversations about this, in which I insisted that all twelve players were to have a share. At the dinner Tony Greig said that he welcomed the money, but that he would much rather we divided it nine ways than not get it at all.

A few years ago Yorkshire bowled Middlesex out for 23 at Headingley. I described the pitch then as a mosaic of green and brown. The Test pitch had a faintly similar look, though it would obviously be infinitely better. Marsh and Chappell looked long and hard at the pitch before we tossed and we speculated that they might have wanted to put us in. They played Bright instead of O'Keeffe – a move which rather weakened their batting. We played Roope instead of Miller.

My part in the day's play is briefly described. I let one go; the next hit my pad: the third was well up just outside off-stump, and I was caught behind. Seeing the action-replay on television I realized what a good ball it was, moving away very late.

The night before, in bed, I had read sketchily the book *Zen in the Art of Archery*, a classic study by the German philosopher, Eugen Herrigel. Training for this art involved doing exercises for a year or more before even shooting an arrow, and the eventual aim is to be able to rid oneself so completely of the striving conscientious ego that the arrow seems to fire itself. Television cameras cannot yet reveal that undigested traces of these ideas were, I am afraid, blundering about in my mind as I went out to bat.

In a room along the corridor there was a more productive sleeplessness. Geoff Boycott, who had been anxious to leave the team dinner for an early night, slept

Boycott in action: a characteristic shot. He forces the ball away off the back foot square on the off side. Notice the foot parallel with the crease, and the head in line with the off stump

for only four hours. He complained about this next morning. If it was not Boycott's night, it was certainly Boycott's day.

He needed all his skill especially against Thomson and Walker, who moved the ball all day despite the hot sun. Walker at times forced him to hurry, and jab down on the ball. Several times, he let the ball go very late as it moved away

Yorkshire's hundred 100s club: It was a great occasion at Headingley, with three of the county's greatest opening batsmen present: Geoffrey Boycott, Herbert Sutcliffe and Sir Leonard Hutton. (Since this caption was written, we had the sad news of Herbert Sutcliffe's death on 21 January 1978. Sir Leonard said of him in the context of this photograph: 'I wouldn't put Herbert down as a classical player, but he had some of Geoff Boycott's characteristics: magnificent temperament and great fighting spirit.')

from him. As usual, he was quick to get into position for what is almost his stock shot, the force off the back foot through cover. At the same time he is still able to lean into the ball on the front foot. Most of us are more committed to one or the other.

This match might almost have been stage-managed. The Yorkshire crowd exuberantly greeted Geoff's 50. Their enthusiasm, on and off the field, reached West Indian proportions. At his 100, they cheered for almost ten minutes; and the weary Australians sat down on the grass. He batted on for another 5 hours, and when he was last out for 191, our total of 436 was virtually unassailable.

All the other main batsmen played useful supporting innings in their own styles, the best being Knott's. Randall was l.b.w. to Pascoe; he thought the ball was missing the leg stump until he saw the action-replay which showed to his surprise how far he had shuffled across.

I have come to admire Australian batsmen for the straightforward way they react to umpires. I had a long chat with Ian Chappell that weekend; he said plainly that he has never 'walked' since a South African fielder held up the ball to claim a catch from him when everyone, except the batsman, knew the ball had bounced; they knew the fielder knew it too. But Ian, like almost all the others – only David Hookes shows his disgruntlement at being given out – always accepted a decision without dissent. He criticized me, rightly, for not looking at the umpire when I was given out in the first over of the match.

However, when fielding, the Australians did show their discontent, even amazement, at a few decisions during the series.

I think that in the field we were more restrained. Again, much of the credit

Knott catching Marsh, brilliantly, off Botham at Headingley. Non-striker Robinson.

for this goes to Tony Greig, for his insistence as captain that we all carried straight on with the game without fuss when a decision went against us. I stressed that this attitude must continue.

Our innings ended at tea on Friday. By the close, Australia had collapsed to 67 for 5, and in only 70 minutes of Saturday were all out for 103. The cloudier weather helped our seam bowlers. No one in the world could have played Hendrick with certainty in these conditions. He is so relaxed these days, he holds the ball so loosely that Willis calls him 'the caresser'. It is hard to analyse just why he had so much more success in this series than Walker, who bowls at much the same pace. I think Hendrick bowled a little straighter and to a fuller length. His stock delivery moves out, though as I've said, he claims not to know which way the ball will move, so there is little point in a batsman trying to 'read' it from his action. I find when I face him that the ball that looks like a half-volley is not that far up. His high action gives him more margin for error in length and gives him valuable bounce.

Botham too bowled very well. He used his in-swinger sparingly, and kept the ball up to the bat. Between them they took nine wickets. The tenth, McCosker's, went to Randall. Hookes pushed a ball towards the gap between

Top: Headingley, 1st innings. Greig about to catch Robinson (at second attempt) off Hendrick.

The most interesting thing here is that Woolmer had just gone from backward short leg to silly mid-off. Robinson had been more or less kicking at the good length ball just outside off-stump, with his bat close behind his leg. This meant that sometimes the ball would brush his pad, then hit his bat and bounce up on the off side. I decided to put in a silly mid-off in the hope that he would drive at the ball and edge it rather than lunge at it with his foot. This is exactly what happened. Greig, unusually, needed two bites at the cherry to make the catch. 3rd slip Willis, 1st slip Brearley, non-striker Bright.

Bottom: Headingley, 1st innings. Walters c. Hendrick b. Botham.

Nice to see six men in the slip and gulley area for England against Australia! The rest of the field was: Randall cover, Boycott mid-wicket, Underwood long leg. The ball swung away, Walters opened up as the ball came and then veered out with his bat, and was well caught by Hendrick. Greig controlled the impulse to grab. Walters was vulnerable in this area, but always liable to score very fast if you have such an attacking field against him. Slips (left to right): Brearley, Greig, Hendrick, Roope, Willis, Woolmer.

Good crowd; clear view of the 'shooting gallery' behind the bowler's arm. This provides a reasonable background, provided the people keep still. The trouble here is that someone as tall as Willis delivers the ball from a height which puts it, from the batsman's point of view, above the shooting gallery, in the trees.

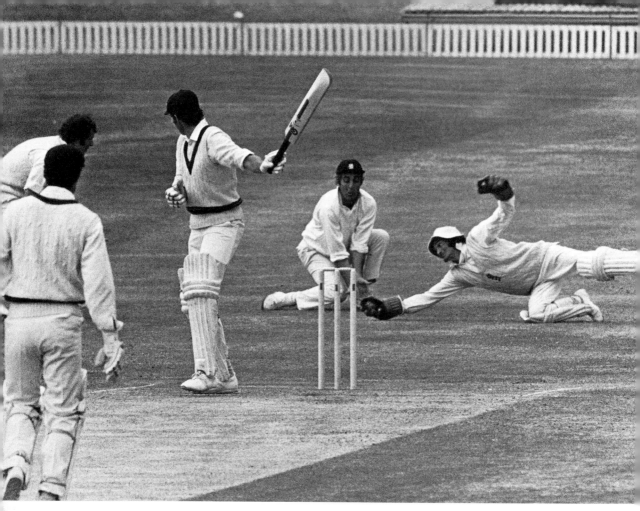

2nd innings.
McCosker c. Knott b.
Greig.
Knott's second
tremendous catch in
this match, very low
and wide.
The ball would not
have carried to me.
Knott practises
catching one-handed
every day. This was
the last over before
lunch, third day,
soon after we changed
the ball. Chappell
non-striker

extra cover (Randall) and the stumps, and took a speculative pace down the wicket. As McCosker responded, but only by a yard or two beyond where his backing-up took him, Randall darted in like quicksilver and with unbelievable quickness threw the wicket down at the bowler's end with McCosker still a yard out.

I had no hesitation about enforcing the follow-on. Our bowlers had only been going for $1\frac{1}{4}$ hours that morning. If Hendrick and Botham tired, we still had Willis, Greig and Woolmer to take advantage of the overcast conditions, as well as Underwood who might occasionally turn the ball on this pitch. There was a rest-day on Sunday.

Willis bowled a much better line in the second innings, working his way in from outside the off stump until he was confident about his line. Davis played neatly; he was unlucky to get out caught down the leg side off Greig. I brought Tony on after a few overs of Hendrick; the commentators were critical, but my view was that he would swing the ball and make it bounce here. Soon after, the ball went out of shape. The umpires ordered play to continue with that ball for a few overs; then they changed it. The replacement, to our surprise, swung more sharply. I remember Greg Chappell standing with his hands on his hips,

2nd innings. Chappell c. Greig b. Willis.

Chappell had been spending half his time between balls with his hands on his hips looking up at the clouds and the bad background, trying to get the umpires to go off for bad light. We had just come out, and though it was cloudy, and though Willis' hand is above the screen, it didn't seem to me to be too dark. He tried to drive, rather as in the first innings when I caught him off Hendrick; the ball was a good length and line, and he didn't quite lean into the ball. In 1953 John Arlott said that the Australians find it more of a disadvantage playing with the inadequate sight-screens in England than the English, who are used to it. It seems to me that it is a false economy to make seating space a higher priority than adequate screens, since bad sightscreens mean more play lost because of bad light (which is always hard to explain to the public) and slower batting (since you can't see the ball clearly enough to play shots).

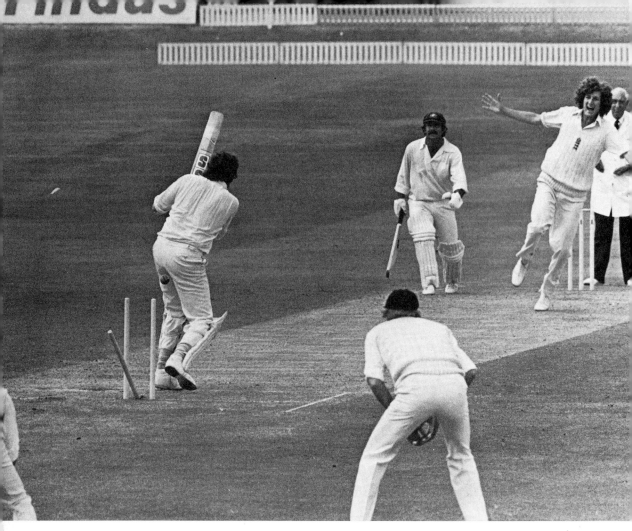

Willis bowls Walker for 30 with the new ball. Just before the end. He and Marsh put on 80 or so; we had been a bit ragged at this point, and had discussions about whether to take the new ball. Fortunately, Willis got everything right straight away, and bowled very quick and straight. Walker is rather ambitious with this stroke – very open and trying to force

incredulous that even this should go against him. Greig rubbed salt into their wounds by having McCosker caught by Knott diving to his right. It was his second masterly catch of the morning.

Chappell survived through the afternoon, but by the time rain stopped play we had seen the backs of Hookes and Walters.

On Monday heavy drizzle and low clouds delayed play until after lunch and, when we started at 2 o'clock, I was a little worried about whether the follow-throughs were safe for our bowlers. But they were all right and when Botham went off, it was because he aggravated his injured foot by stepping on a ball in the field. It remained overcast and Greg Chappell, hands on his hips again, kept fussing about the light and the sight screens. He must have been half-thinking of the light when Willis had him caught at second slip for 36 trying to drive. Now that Chappell was gone, the chances of Australia winning or saving the match were remote unless it poured with rain.

It did not. On the contrary, it brightened and our next frustration came when Walker and Marsh joined in an awkward stand. Runs came fairly fast, Marsh either playing-and-missing or hitting fours, Walker heaving two of his own off

Underwood. That ragged feeling was settling in. At about twenty minutes to tea, the new ball became due. Greig, Knott and I were of three different persuasions. Greig thought it was dangerous to take it because it might go faster off the bat; the old ball was still swinging and we could not know whether the new ball would swing or not. He thought we should carry on. Knott thought we should continue with the seamers whether or not we took the new ball. I thought we should take the new ball because at least that would have that extra pace, that extra fire in it. The other ball had lost some of its bounce. I decided to take the new ball. As it happened, Willis bowled really quickly straightaway, as he had done earlier in the day. In his first over he bowled Walker off his pad and Thomson the next ball but one, so there were nine down. The next over Marsh had his slog against Hendrick and the fifth ball of that over was the ball that won the Ashes.

10 Confrontations

Kerry Packer, who had already signed forty-six first-class players for his Super-Tests, arrived from Australia to see the Fourth Test. He was in England also to prepare his High Court case, protect his interests (Jeff Thomson withdrew from the camp a fortnight earlier), and perhaps increase his signings. He was staying in Leeds at the same hotel as the England team.

I had met Kerry Packer only once, at Edgbaston early in June. He did not have a bone-crushing handshake. Tony Greig introduced us. 'Get a few hundreds,' he said to me, 'and you might see more of each other.'

I did not see him again until the Headingley Test. On Sunday evening, after a relaxing day with friends, I was asked over to join his dinner party. I had eaten, so I just drank some coffee, before going up to bed. At about 11 p.m., when I was in my night-shirt and dressing gown, Tony came to my room to see if I would go and talk privately with Kerry Packer in his room. Tony and Ian Chappell were there too.

We talked for a while about Packer's plans. I asked him why he had insisted on a definite answer about television rights at the ICC meeting, when it seemed to me that it was the Australian Board which would have to decide this matter, not the ICC. Packer then gave me his version of the history of the dispute. He clearly was not prepared to wait for the outcome of a process of putting in tenders for the rights to televise cricket in Australia. As Mr Justice Slade said, the parties had an irreconcilable difference of approach.

Then he said 'Let's come to the point. What do you think of the idea of me signing up the whole England team? As you know I've got the West Indians and the Australian team and what I would like to see is if the full England team could take on the full Australian team with the Chappells and Lillee. What a tremendous bill!'

I hedged. 'From what point of view, what do I think of the idea?' It struck me as odd if he thought I could answer for players other than myself. It also struck me that without the captain there could be no 'whole' England team. Was this an academic question?

'Come on,' he said, 'would you do it?'

'No,' I replied. I had of course like other Test players considered the possibility of being invited. I had decided that I did not want to join, let alone recruit.

The conversation became more general again. Tony and I both stressed that we did not want head-on confrontation between Packer and the TCCB. I mentioned the Middlesex move towards a Cricketers' Association meeting, and suggested that Packer might talk to the Association's representatives. (This meeting took place at the Dorchester on the following Tuesday.)

We also knew that David Evans was very keen to organize an initiative towards compromise. Packer was willing to discuss any move, so we also decided to ask Evans to come to Leeds the next evening.

With mind racing, I went back to bed. Next day we won the Ashes. At 8 p.m., the same four men gathered again in Kerry Packer's room. By the time Evans arrived, at 9 o'clock, the room was cluttered with enormous trollies covered with the debris of steak sandwiches, ice buckets, bottles of beer and fizzy drinks. Post-Test languour had set in; the room became a den. Ties were loosened and jackets discarded.

At first Evans was disregarded. He looked as much at home as a stockbroker in a transport cafe. It was Tony who reminded everyone that David had come a long way and had an idea of importance. Evans and Packer had liked each other at their only meeting. They both reckoned they understood each other. His proposal was that Packer should join a consortium of businessmen who were determined to support first-class cricket in England. Packer had no real quarrel with English cricket, yet they were heading for all-out war. If the TCCB saw that Packer was prepared, whether privately or publicly, to help the financing of the Test matches of 1978, might they not postpone their ban on his players for a year? I was in favour of such a moratorium. I suggested that perhaps, too, Packer would agree not to sign any more England players during this period.

Packer did not respond to that; perhaps he had already decided to invite Willis, Woolmer and Randall to join him. He was prepared to offer a financial inducement to have the ban called off. He told Evans that if the TCCB accepted such an offer, they would have an extra £50,000, and no expensive law-suit. For a year, negotiations could go on.

Evans went away to put the proposal to the TCCB. None of us was sanguine. I felt that the TCCB would not be persuaded by an offer of money; the fundamental argument between the two worlds could be summed up in the Australian Board's horror at Packer's saying 'Come, gentlemen, there's a bit of the whore in all of us when it comes to money.' Moreover, the English authorities would feel that a year's time would mean a year in which he could strengthen his position.

The die had been cast. Evans' plan found no favourable response.

Why did I say No to Packer's offer, or at least not listen further? It would be hypocritical to suggest that the financial consequences were irrelevant. I suppose that I might have been offered up to £20,000 a year for two or three years, whether or not the Super-Test series survived.

On the other hand, after years of county cricket at a modest captain's salary which began at £1,760 in 1971 and reached £3,400 in 1977, I had been granted a

There was a law suit –
and it was expensive.
Here Kerry Packer and
Tony Greig arrive for
the first day of the
hearing

benefit for 1978. It is public knowledge that benefits can earn up to £20,000, but rarely over £30,000. The rewards for Test cricket are improving, thanks partly to Packer himself, but naturally one has no security of tenure.

Money apart, Kerry Packer is not my style. England is my home. I prefer the chugging British coaster with a cargo of pig-iron to a monstrous Supertanker hurriedly constructed. We put up with the buckets to catch the drips in the dressing-room at Taunton in order to enjoy the wisteria round the door of The George at Bewley. I like the regional rivalries that inform our game. I have relished the challenge of the captaincy of Middlesex and England.

I am wary of the role television can play in cricket. Even the John Player Sunday League, while a necessary source of income and the scene of much exciting cricket, is to some extent a package for television, as bowlers' run-ups are restricted to ensure that forty overs can be fitted into the programme. I am afraid that if cricket is to adapt to television, rather than the other way round, the whole rhythm of the game that has developed organically will be destroyed.

Individually, some of Packer's innovations are impressive. Collectively, they are dangerously experimental. I like the idea of his sight-screens, which could be seen through by the spectator but would present a massive plain background for the batsman. Night cricket *may* work, though night baseball in America has been found to shorten a player's career owing to eye-strain.

As I write, in November 1977, no one knows whether an adequate pitch can be grown in a greenhouse and laid in a trough in the middle of a field. It may work. As an alternative to the orthodox and well-tried, such an experiment would be valuable. But as the *only* possibility, it is extremely risky. If I were to face Lillee and Holding under floodlights on an experimental pitch I should want a suit of armour, not just a helmet.

I do not like the idea of drawing circles round the wickets and restricting the number of fielders allowed outside them. It savours of artificially induced aggression. Nor am I keen on microphones being planted near the stumps. Temperamentally I am for reform not for revolution. I hope that the influence of people like Greig and the Chappells will be strong enough to prevent the 'bit of a whore' becoming wholesale prostitution.

People ask me if I think the new cricket will succeed. I don't know. Much depends on whether the public identify with the official Australia Test side or with Mr Packer's Australian XI. I do not think that the mere stamp of official approval will guarantee public support, nor, for that matter, will the presence of most of the world's finest cricketers guarantee substantial crowds.

Nor can I see that the ban on players from first-class cricket is either fair or sensible. The likelihood of a ban did not discourage Woolmer and Amiss from signing for Packer. Woolmer's reasons included his resentment that Kent did not support their players by opposing the ban. It is not clear to me that Packer's cricket is such a threat to the established game as to justify banning Underwood, for example, from playing for Kent when all he has done is to sign a contract for the period when Kent do not employ him.

Moreover, the costs risked by the TCCB in laying themselves open to Packer's suit were costs that the counties – and therefore the players – cannot afford. Admittedly, Packer's early secrecy led to the whole scheme being sprung on an amazed cricketing world. It made confrontation almost inevitable. But cricket's administrators have never succeeded in organizing the game so that the players receive a reasonable income.

This subject has been hammered to death in the Press and the law courts, but no account of the controversy is complete without it. Take Underwood again: in the year April 1976–March 1977, he told me, he earned from cricket £7,600. He played in 11 Tests. He is, of course, at the height of his profession. He is a Lord

Olivier of cricket, but his career will not extend into his 70s. He has a family, from whom he was away for seven months of that busy year. This separation was one of the main factors persuading Greg Chappell to retire from Test cricket.

Cricket, or at least Test cricket, is not an entertainment backwater. Large crowds watched the West Indies in England in 1976. In India, a million or more watched the five Tests, and perhaps another $\frac{3}{4}$ million the rest of the Tour. In Australia, $\frac{1}{4}$ million watched the Centenary Test. In addition to these cheering, jeering masses there are the invisible, inaudible watchers and readers.

If Underwood needs an infra-structure to support him, so does Olivier. No one would blame him – or for that matter a surgeon or a journalist – for considering a handsome offer to join a new experiment with the outstanding practitioners in his field.

Opponents of Packer have said they agree that Test players were badly paid. But it took a radical innovation to make them act on it. It took Packer to produce, via Evans, the Cornhill sponsorship which will mean, amongst other things, much improved payments for Test matches.

County cricketers are more precariously placed. By a small majority they voted to support the ban, so clearly a majority feel that Packer threatens our interests. Yet since the 1930s the lot of the cricketer has deteriorated relative to many others'.

In 1938, a capped player for Derbyshire would earn £325 a year. At that time, a labourer would earn about £120–130 a year; a schoolteacher, starting his career with a first-class degree and a teaching certificate, £248. In the mid-thirties, an average British freighter master could expect a salary of £28–35 *a month*, and long leave was practically unheard of.

In 1977, an average capped player for Derbyshire earned about £2,500, well below the national average outside cricket. Apart from Lancashire, I doubt any county paid their top players (excluding a few captains) more than £3,500: many paid much less. Middlesex had their most successful season in history, considering all the competitions (quarter-finalists of the Benson and Hedges Cup, 3rd in the John Player League, winners of the Gillette Cup, and joint winners of the Schweppes County Championship). Yet a top player who played in all the matches received about £4,000, including prize money. Getting and spending may lay waste our powers, but the inability to get it may lay waste county cricket. The benefit makes some players' careers worthwhile. But a benefit is not part of a contract; only 25 per cent of those playing full-time ever get one.

Packer did not have to use much persuasion to attract his players. His case is that cricket has been undersold. Certainly it is absurd that in 1977 a county member could watch every home match from the best seats for only £10 a year; for that money, he could see 49 days' cricket.

The fundamental difficulty is that so few people watch county cricket, though thanks to the TCCB's far-sightedness in the mid-sixties, more spectators come now than then. The crucial questions are: Can English cricket afford so extended a substructure of 3-day county cricket with 17 counties? Is there a fixed income for cricket so that if Packer takes the cream the milk is thinner for everyone else? Or is he showing others how undersold cricket has been?

I do not know the answers to these questions, nor do I have any special access to knowledge about the future. I am not wildly attracted to the image of either mode – to the dark suit and striped tie of the establishment or to the snappy cerise with crocodile-skin shoes of the alternative society. My style is more informal than either.

One's commitments and loyalties are formed partly by accident and partly by choice. My choice was to stay in county cricket. I should like to help Middlesex and I hope England succeed, and play cricket the right way. But I should also like to contribute towards an atmosphere in which there is flexibility and the possibility of compromise.

February 1978. Most of what I wrote in November holds good. New developments will quickly outdate any account, but it seems worthwhile to write briefly about the main events of the winter so far. The balance sheet looks even. Packer won the law-suit, but his three players, sent to Karachi in January for the Third Test between Pakistan and England, were not allowed to play. Packer had success with some of his night matches, but the Australian public preferred the Tests against India to his Super-Tests.

Though both sides have much to gain from a compromise, feelings have hardened. I was against the ban on players, but I was never in favour of Packer's players coming in and out of Test teams as it suited them (or him). England can have no continuity, no steady team spirit, if Knott, Greig and the others are selected to play in the home series in 1978. New loyalties arise. The England team expressed this general attitude very forcibly at Karachi, firstly with a statement, and then by announcing that they would not play if Zaheer, Mushtaq and Imran were selected. My own part in that drama was abruptly stopped by the freak ball from Sikander Bakht which broke my arm and required me to return to England for immediate treatment.

At county level the situation is different. Hampshire have just announced that they have retained their Packer players, and Kent have offered terms to Asif, Knott, Underwood and Woolmer. Wayne Daniel is not, as far as we know, precluded from any Middlesex matches because of his World Series contract, so he has not in any sense let Middlesex down by his winter activities. Most senior players want him to play for us. The club indicated to him last September that, if the ban failed, we would be keen to have him back. Finally, he would be justified in suing for unjustified dismissal if we did not offer him another contract. So, legally, morally and prudentially, Middlesex have good reason to engage Wayne Daniel. I imagine other counties will take a similar line.

11 Anticlimax at the Oval

The Fifth Test

Middlesex, meanwhile, had fallen from the lead in the County Championship and, having missed more matches than in any season since I became captain, I felt frustrated and anxious about the team. There had been reports of injuries in the side and they had lost two matches during the Headingley Test. Now they were about to lose to Northamptonshire, so I visited Wellingborough to discuss the problems with Mike Smith. The injured players were all fit by the next day, when we were meant to play Somerset in the semi-final of the Gillette Cup at Lord's. Then the rains came.

You don't get much rest when it's raining, especially if you are captain in a tense match. There were discussions about rearranging the Championship match with Somerset, scheduled for the next week, so as to fit in the Gillette Cup semi-final. Somerset, however, didn't want it played at the end of the season because they were going off to Jersey. We could not have Lord's during the other available space and did not want to play on a Middlesex club ground because no pitch that might last three days could be prepared at less than a week's notice. Eventually, we agreed to play at the only other available grounds, which were Birmingham or Chelmsford. Birmingham often produces draws, and we could not afford a draw, so we picked Chelmsford, where at least the ball does something. It kept raining. The Oval Test, which started the following week, was an anticlimax, partly because this series was already over, and partly because of the weather.

One spot of joy in the gloom was the decision of the selectors, by then unanimous, to include Packer players who had contributed so richly to England's successful summer. Thus at that time, it seemed that Knott was to finish his England career with 88 appearances, Underwood with 71 and Greig with 55. Woolmer had news for me. He, too, was almost certain to sign and would then be ruled out of the forthcoming tour to Pakistan and New Zealand. Randall and Willis had also received offers.

The ground was too wet for play. My first task of the morning was to try to organize a different hotel for the players. They were fed up after a night in noisy rooms and a morning of long queues for breakfast. The Surrey secretary was most helpful, and we managed to find a better place.

I then sought out Woolmer, Willis and Randall.

I tried to steer a fair course of persuasion. Obviously, I wanted them to continue playing for England. Equally obviously, each had to make up his own mind, and the alternatives appear differently to each individual. My advice was always: find out, before you decide, what the likeliest consequences will be;

John Lever at the Oval. I wouldn't have picked it up!

listen to people opposed to Packer as well as to those who are committed to him.

The match started a day late and through much of the morning I faced Mick Malone, who had come in for Pascoe who was still injured. Now and then I glanced at the clouds gathered over the river to the north. At Lord's, Middlesex were playing Somerset in the semi-final of the Gillette Cup, a match reduced to 15 overs. We had been waiting five days to play it and reports over the loudspeaker at the Oval kept us informed of the score. Middlesex finally took the match by lunchtime.

Malone, in his Test debut, carried the day. A workhorse, he bowled all but two of the overs bowled from the Vauxhall end that day. He ended with five wickets for 63 runs off 47 overs. Malone is a big, strong physical education teacher from Perth, an Australian Rules footballer. His high action was hard to pick up against the background of the temporary stand. There was a gangway just at the top of the bowler's arm and the ball came out of this, through the

Roope batting at the Oval. Well forward to Thomson or Walker. A fine stroke-maker, Roope played the moving ball better than most in this match

black and into the glaring white below. Boycott and I both batted just under three hours for 39 on an extremely slow pitch.

It wasn't until after Walker came on at about 12.15 that the ball started to swing more and more sharply, and the shine came up remarkably. The television commentators, I understand, claimed he was rubbing grease on his face, then onto the ball. It looked a bit odd to me, too, from the non-striker's end, and as the day wore on, Malone's shirt became bright red. I had a word with the umpire and we watched Walker as he went back to his mark, but these things are hard to prove. It is an incident worth mentioning but certainly not worth blowing up into a controversy such as the one we suffered over Lever in India.

One other interesting incident came in the second innings. I had got out early to Thomson with my worst shot of the season, getting my head too far over for an unexpectedly lifting ball and fending it off to short leg. Boycott was in a stand with Randall, struggling in the fading light. As a ball was being bowled to Geoff, mid-wicket dropped back about thirty yards and fine leg went round twenty yards. I think some of the movement happened after the bowler started his run-up. Malone then bowled a bouncer in the hope that Boycott would hit it in the air and get caught, which very nearly happened.

Oval. End of Greg Chappell's Test career. Caught and bowled Underwood 39. Left to right: Knott, McCosker, Spencer (umpire), Underwood, Brearley, Greig. Chappell played his favourite on-drive (Knott is taking the ball just by the leg stump), the ball was not quite far enough up, turned slightly, and went off a thick outside-edge, back to the bowler

Boycott was cross. There is only one way to stop this tactic and that is for the non-striker to be extremely alert and stop the bowler as he is running in to bowl when he sees the fielders are changing positions. It is the batsman's job to see the field when the bowler starts but, thereafter, it is the non-striker's responsibility. It was a good point Geoff raised and it illustrates not only his own total concentration but that he expects the same of his batting partner.

It was fitting that Boycott, after such a glorious return to England cricket, was batting when the day, the match, and the series petered out in bad light. He now is one of 14 batsmen to score 5,000 runs in Test cricket and his remarkable average of 147·33 for the series beat Bradman's Ashes record of 139·14, which he set in 1930. Another notable record was gained by Willis, who chose to continue in Test and county cricket rather than join Packer. Willis slept better, kept fit and knocked over 27 wickets in the series, the highest in history by an England quick bowler against Australia.

For the most part, it was a ragged, wet game, one that lacked the keen edge of competition. They dropped catches. We dropped more than we did in any match through the series. Even Greig, the best slip-fielder I've ever played with, dropped one. It was the first slip catch I saw him drop since the start of the Indian tour.

The Australians scored their highest score of the series, 385, and I was surprised they did not declare at lunchtime that last day. I think Chappell was a little resigned by now and he let his tail-enders slog on, rather than trying to bowl us out and win the Test match. We thus went through the five matches without a declaration being made against us. Even the manner of Chappell's dismissal put a kind of full stop to his visit. Dropped by Underwood in his first innings, he was caught by Underwood in his last.

But once again the Australian captain was gracious when he came out onto the balcony for television. 'We've been beaten by a better side and we're quite happy to admit it,' he said. 'It doesn't do any harm to see the other side of the fence. It puts the game into true perspective.'

12 Perspectives

After the summer was over I had lunch with Sir Leonard Hutton, who was captain the last time England recaptured the Ashes at home and, among many questions, I asked him who of the Australians might have got into the Australian side his team beat in 1953. 'Only one man,' he replied, 'and that was Greg Chappell.'

I am not qualified to evaluate the team that toured England that summer but I share his admiration for Chappell. He has superb bearing on the field; whatever he does he looks graceful. I cannot remember him playing an ungainly shot. Even when he was almost hit by one of Willis' bouncers at Manchester he turned the hasty evasion into a gymnastic recovery. He has an excellent defence, and plays every stroke. When he was at the crease, Australia always had a chance. One main factor in our success was our ability to contain Chappell. In eight of his nine Test innings, often frustrated by the accuracy of our bowling, he was out to an attacking stroke.

No doubt Chappell was frustrated also by the degree of responsibility he continually carried. By the end of the summer he yawned frequently on the field. We were surprised that he bowled so little; perhaps he could not face yet another task, or perhaps bowling jarred an ankle that seemed to trouble him from time to time. Early in the tour, he once or twice showed his exasperation with other players on the field; by the end of the tour he seemed less engaged, less exacting, more resigned.

There were rumours of difficulties within the Australian camp during the tour. Four of their seventeen players – Serjeant, Cosier, Dymock and Hughes – were not contracted to Packer. Perhaps this was a source of conflict. All I can say is that no sign of it was visible to me. Len Maddocks, the manager, a member of the Australian Board of Control, was presumably aghast to find out that three-quarters of his team had, secretly, committed themselves to the Board's fiercest enemy. The discovery, whether or not learned from the newspapers, cannot have made his job any easier.

However, it is sheer speculation to say that Packer's spectral presence contributed to Australia's defeat. I was irritated by the frequent, facile suggestions to this effect. My own experience is that it is hard to link external events with performance on the field. It would be implausible to suggest that Knott, Greig and Underwood played below their best, or that the team-spirit in the England dressing-room was disrupted because of the controversy. One side had to lose; the result may equally have been no different if Mr Packer had never been born. I am sure that Chappell and his side set out as would any other

'Tangles' Walker at Lord's.

The nickname could come from the action or the signature, or from his entertaining tangle of words. He is an architect: I wonder if his buildings look like his writing. By no means a classical action; he's looking inside his left arm, his chest facing the batsman. It is not unlike Bob Willis' action. Max is not as upright or as high as, say, Thomson or Old would be at this point just before delivery, and he has to lose some momentum to get into this jack-knife position. But Walker is about 6′ 4″, he must weigh 16 stone, and he's very strong indeed. He was a successful Australian-rules footballer, so he's got to the top in two professional sports as well as being a qualified architect. Notice the cocked wrist which enables him to bowl the in-swinger and the leg-cutter, both of which are natural deliveries.

I think he was the unluckiest bowler in the series. Perhaps he bowled marginally too short, and at times too wide; but he could easily have bowled exactly as he did and have taken twice as many wickets. I found him harder to play than anyone.

Above: England at the Oval: *left to right: back row:* D. W. Randall, R. A. Woolmer, M. Hendrick, R. G. D. Willis, G. R. J. Roope, J. K. Lever; *front row:* D. L. Underwood, G. Boycott, J. M. Brearley, A. W. Grcig, A. P. E. Knott.

Below: The other members of the England Test teams: *left to right:* C. M. Old, D. L. Amiss, G. Miller, G. D. Barlow, I. T. Botham. (Oval photograph by courtesy of Sport and General)

self-respecting team, saying, in effect, 'if this is our last fling, let's show them'.

Chappell himself I have discussed; his batting was outstanding, and this narrative shows how well I think we bowled at him. Marsh and Walker played in their utterly whole-hearted ways. Marsh was clearly one of the most dangerous of Australia's batsmen, and we did well to dismiss him cheaply so often. He kept wicket superbly. Walker's length was perhaps marginally short, but with more luck, he might have taken twice as many wickets bowling the same way. He was the bowler I least enjoyed facing, because he swings the ball so sharply and gets it to bounce.

Thomson and McCosker made remarkable recoveries from disastrous injuries. Thomson bowled well, though only in the Second Test at his quickest. We expected more short-pitched deliveries from him, and wondered whether his shoulder still hurt him. McCosker's courage is remarkable. At Nottingham, with his second innings 107, he had clearly overcome the confidence-shattering jaw break he suffered at Melbourne.

Walters has never made many runs in England, and by the end of the tour he probably did not want ever to play here again. For him, the watershed must have been that full-toss at Old Trafford, when he was only twelve short of a century.

Their other batsmen were disappointing. Hookes is a beautiful timer of the ball, but loose. Robinson looked out of his depth against Test bowling. Davis, with some pleasing innings, played better than the figures suggest. Serjeant's first innings promised much, as did some of Hughes' early performances. But the batting as a whole was vulnerable.

O'Keeffe was one of the hardest to get out. His bowling returns must have been disappointing, though he did not bowl badly. I suppose Australia never scored enough runs for their leg-spinner to be most useful. Leg-spinners can be scored off on both sides of the wicket, since they bowl leg-breaks, googlies and top-spinners; the sheer physical contortions they have to go through means that they will rarely be as hard to score off as an orthodox finger-spinner. In the Centenary Test, he bowled 36 overs and took four important wickets; but there our target was 445. A leg-spinner is more dependent on the side's batting for his own performance than anyone else. Pascoe and Malone have been described earlier. They were two of the successes of the tour.

Overall, the most striking difference between the sides lay in the fielding, and especially in the close catching. I have described our practice: it contrasts with the typical methods employed, for example, in Hutton's day when, he said, 'four or five of us would hit a ball up, sky it, hitting it so you had to run a bit'.

Slip cradles were used then, of course; but my impression is that catching practice was haphazard. Dropped catches have incalculable effects on how fresh a bowler is for a new batsman, on bowlers' morale, on the buoyance of the whole team. It is a terrible feeling to stand in the slips and hope that a catch does

The Australian Touring Team 1977: *left to right: back row:* S. P. McRae (masseur), R. J. Bright, K. Hughes, R. D. Robinson, G. Cosier, M. F. Malone, D. W. Hookes, C. S. Serjeant, G. Dymock, L. S. Pascoe, D. K. Sherwood (scorer); *front row:* L. V. Maddocks (manager), K. J. O'Keeffe, R. B. McCosker, K. D. Walters, G. S. Chappell, R. W. Marsh, M. H. N. Walker, J. R. Thomson, I. C. Davis, N. T. McMahon (treasurer)

not come your way.

Catching apart, the sides were not so different as the scores suggest. Our batting was perhaps more dogged and determined than theirs. Fortunately Woolmer's main successes occurred when they were most needed, before Boycott returned. That meant that in each of the first four Tests, at least one batsman played a major innings, which guaranteed a good total to bowl at.

Our bowlers were superb. We had more depth here than the Australians. We always had three front-line seam bowlers, with Greig and Woolmer to back them up. All Greig's seven victims were specialist batsmen. Willis' improvement has been described; one aspect of it was that eight of his twenty-seven wickets were tail-enders. Underwood, too, usefully wrapped up the innings for us. He is a unique bowler; some of his tussles with Chappell provided fascinating cricket. Hendrick, Old, Botham, and Lever could all be relied on to bowl accurately and to move the ball if conditions allowed. We were able to keep pressure on Australia most of the time.

Team spirit is, of course, an intangible commodity. It contributes to success and is helped by success. Ours was already excellent at the beginning of the

Placing the field during the Fourth Test. The batsman is Ian Davis

series. The winter tour ended with a happy side which enjoyed playing together. Much of the credit for this, and for the victory against Australia, belongs to Tony Greig. When he was dismissed as captain, he might have shown more resentment, or have been only moderately cooperative. In fact, he could not have been more helpful. He and I dined together during the Tests. During the summer we became closer, personally, than we had been during the four months abroad.

Traditionally, cricketers have been sceptical about the value of team meetings and tactical talks. As Hutton said, 'You can have all sorts of fancy ideas and then in the game you might as well throw them out the window.' There is often, too, a certain shyness about semi-formal discussions. Cricketers, rightly, are pragmatic; flexibility is essential. However, people *do* query policies, they *do* have ideas of their own.

Social changes have affected cricket dressing-rooms. Younger players are more outspoken than when I started. They are less likely to refrain from telling jokes directed at senior players. Fifteen years ago, the prevailing attitude was that you did not voice an opinion on tactics until you had played in about twenty Test matches. I have known fine players 'go grey in the service of the game' (in Ranjitsinhji's phrase) without thinking about tactics or about other peoples' jobs and problems.

A captain needs to find a balance between utilizing the knowledge of his colleagues and retaining the final say. My two winters working in a therapeutic community for disturbed adolescents helped me in all this. At the clinic I was excited to be in a place where everyone had a say in discussions and ideas. As junior members of staff, we could – and did – challenge the senior members and clearly influenced the way the clinic was run. At the same time, I saw that confusion about the decision-making process can be irritating if, for example, a

The dressing-room, the Oval. I was asking Geoff for his ideas about the team for Pakistan and New Zealand. In the foreground are some of the bats I was getting autographed for my benefit in 1978

discussion about how to deal with a particular situation turns out to be merely abstract since the decision has already been made.

A captain has to take responsibility for what he does. He must act, and often he must decide on the spur of the moment. My ideal is to be, often, authoritarian on the field and much more democratic off it. At Middlesex, we now have a side in which at various stages everyone will come up with ideas, not only about cricket but also about the running of the club. On the field, players accept what I do.

The risk of too much discussion is loss of decisiveness. It is not surprising that people sometimes yearn for the older, simpler structures of authority. However, I'm convinced that consultation, done in the right way, leads to more constructive leadership and is a sign not of weakness but of strength.

Captains must accept criticism. Soon after I became captain Mike Smith said to me, 'that's not a crown on you head, that's a coconut'. You have to accept this. People like to have heroes and villains, they prefer white and black to shades of grey.

Too often commentators indulge in what the Americans call 'second-guessing'. Tactical decisions are 'vindicated' by short-term results. Everyone, including the captain, forgets that any alternative decision might have been *more* successful. A move is 'proved wrong'; people forget that any other option may have 'proved worse'. Criticism, and praise, should be based on the probabilities as they were when the decision was made.

I try to enjoy the praise – often as undeserved as the criticism – and to ignore most of the blame. I remember the advice that Renford Bambrough, my Cambridge philosophy supervisor, gave me before I gave a philosophy paper for the first time, at the University of Oregon. He said that it is all too easy to take remarks as more hostile than they are, and it is often best to respond to the hostile ones as if they were not.

In the summer of 1977, I was kindly, sometimes flatteringly, treated. It was, for me, an amazingly exciting year. There was not much time for relaxation. The day after a Test was usually the scene of a vital Gillette Cup match or an equally crucial game in the Championship. The Test series ended in anticlimax, but not the county season. Four days after the Oval Test we beat Glamorgan in the Gillette Cup Final. The Middlesex outfielding was marvellous; better, I think, than England's. (The slip fielding was not as good.) I was out to the first ball of our innings, but Clive Radley played a characteristically determined knock. Our win did not prevent the songs of the valleys resounding round Lord's.

Next day, we travelled to Maidstone. Despite a century from Asif, we batted well enough at this beautiful ground to grab third place in the John Player League. In this match I saw Paul Downton keep wicket for the first time. Two days earlier we had selected him for the tour.

Finally, the next Tuesday, 7 September, we drove to Blackpool. We had to win to have a chance of the Championship. The erratic weather, which had played such a part throughout the season, nearly thwarted us, but by 3.30 p.m. on the last day, Phil Edmonds and John Emburey had bowled us to a win. Soon the news came through that Gloucestershire had lost. Our car radios told us that Brown and Perryman were holding out against Kent. With less than a hour of the season left, Jarvis had Perryman, caught by Woolmer at slip. Kent shared the title with us.

Those journeys down the motorway seem shorter when you've won but I remember some of them with not unqualified pleasure. As I drove back from Leeds after we had won the Ashes I noticed a distinctly unpleasant smell percolating through from the boot. The grouse! After a few miles my stomach could take it no more. I stopped. His Grace's grouse had to go. It was even worse after Blackpool. I had had four days of the gastric flu (as bad as Delhi belly). Every hour we had to stop while I retched beside the road. Success may not fill emotional voids, but in this case it created an intestinal one.

So the season ended. I had not finished *Anna Karenina*. I had chosen my Desert Island Discs and wanted, now, to choose the desert island. For cricket the summer of 1977 was a dividing line in the history of the game. For me, the changes involve loss, the most important being the possible break-up of the England team. I would miss Greig, Knott, Underwood, Amiss and Woolmer as colleagues and friends.

Change also implies gain. New players will emerge. On 24 November my ex-colleagues began their first Packer game in Melbourne. On the same day, the new England side flew out of Heathrow for the tour of Pakistan and New Zealand.

Appendix of Statistics

*Daily close-of-play scores for 1977 England–Australia Test Series,
first-class averages for Test players, final 1977 Test averages,
and Test career averages.*

Appendix of Statistics

First Test
Lord's

FIRST DAY (Thursday 16 June)

England – 1st Innings

				FALL OF WICKETS
AMISS D.L.		b Thomson	4	1–12
BREARLEY J.M.	c Robinson	b Thomson	9	2–13
WOOLMER R.A.	run	out	79	8–183
RANDALL D.W.	c Chappell	b Walker	53	3–111
GREIG A.W.		b Pascoe	5	4–121
BARLOW G.D.	c McCosker	b Walker	1	5–134
KNOTT A.P.E.	c Walters	b Thomson	8	6–155
OLD C.M.	c Marsh	b Walker	9	7–171
LEVER J.K.		b Pascoe	8	9–189
UNDERWOOD D.L.	not	out	11	
WILLIS R.G.D.		b Thomson	17	10–216
EXTRAS (B – 1, LB – 3, NB – 7, W – 1)			12	
		TOTAL	216	

Bowling

	OVERS	MDNS.	RUNS	WKTS.
Thomson	20·5	5	41	4
Pascoe	23	7	53	2
Walker	30	6	66	3
O'Keeffe	10	3	32	0
Chappell	3	0	12	0

Left: First Test, first day: Woolmer forces O'Keeffe

SECOND DAY (Friday 17 June)

England – First Innings 216

Australia – 1st Innings

				FALL OF WICKETS
ROBINSON R.D.		b Lever	11	1–25
MCCOSKER R.B.	not	out	23	
CHAPPELL G.S.	not	out	11	
EXTRAS (LB – 1, NB – 5)			6	
TOTAL (one wicket)			51	

Bowling

	OVERS	MDNS.	RUNS	WKTS.
Willis	6·3	0	24	0
Lever	4	0	14	1
Underwood	6	4	4	0
Old	8	5	3	0

THIRD DAY (Saturday 18 June)

England – First Innings 216

Australia – 1st Innings

				FALL OF WICKETS
ROBINSON R.D.		b Lever	11	1–25
MCCOSKER R.B.		b Old	23	2–51
CHAPPELL G.S.	c Old	b Willis	66	3–135
SERJEANT C.S.	c Knott	b Willis	81	4–238
WALTERS K.D.	c Brearley	b Willis	53	5–256
HOOKES D.W.	c Brearley	b Old	11	6–264
MARSH R.W.	l.b.w.	b Willis	1	7–265
O'KEEFFE K.J.	not	out	8	
WALKER M.H.N.	not	out	1	
EXTRAS (LB – 7, NB – 15, W – 1)			23	
TOTAL (seven wickets)			278	

Bowling

	OVERS	MDNS.	RUNS	WKTS.
Willis	24	5	74	4
Lever	19	5	61	1
Underwood	25	6	42	0
Old	29	9	58	2
Woolmer	5	1	20	0

John Lever about to bowl at Old Trafford. Umpire, Tom Spencer

FOURTH DAY (Monday 20 June)

England – First Innings 216

Australia – 1st Innings

				FALL OF WICKETS
ROBINSON R.D.		b Lever	11	1–25
MCCOSKER R.B.		b Old	23	2–51
CHAPPELL G.S.	c Old	b Willis	66	3–135
SERJEANT C.S.	c Knott	b Willis	81	4–238
WALTERS K.D.	c Brearley	b Willis	53	5–256
HOOKES D.W.	c Brearley	b Old	11	6–264
MARSH R.W.	l.b.w.	b Willis	1	7–265
O'KEEFFE K.J.	c sub. (Ealham)	b Willis	12	9–290
WALKER M.H.N.	c Knott	b Willis	4	8–284
THOMSON J.R.		b Willis	6	10–296
PASCOE L.S.	not	out	3	
EXTRAS (LB – 7, NB – 17, W – 1)			25	
		TOTAL	296	

Bowling

	OVERS	MDNS.	RUNS	WKTS.
Willis	30·1	7	78	7
Lever	19	5	61	1
Underwood	25	6	42	0
Old	35	10	70	2
Woolmer	5	1	20	0

England – 2nd Innings

				FALL OF WICKETS
AMISS D.L.		b Thompson	0	1–0
BREARLEY J.M.	c Robinson	b O'Keeffe	49	2–132
WOOLMER R.A.	not	out	114	
GREIG A.W.	not	out	18	
EXTRAS (B – 5, LB – 2, W – 1)			8	
		TOTAL (two wickets)	189	

Bowling

	OVERS	MDNS.	RUNS	WKTS.
Thomson	13	3	45	1
Pascoe	17	2	56	0
Walker	18	7	38	0
Chappell	7	2	17	0
O'Keeffe	15	7	26	1

First Test, fourth day: Marsh
attempts to run out Woolmer

FIFTH DAY (Tuesday 21 June)

England – First Innings 216

Australia – First Innings 296

England – 2nd Innings

				FALL OF WICKETS
AMISS D.L.		b Thomson	0	1–0
BREARLEY J.M.	c Robinson	b O'Keeffe	49	2–132
WOOLMER R.A.	c Chappell	b Pascoe	120	3–224
GREIG A.W.	c O'Keeffe	b Pascoe	91	5–286
BARLOW G.D.	l.b.w.	b Pascoe	5	4–263
KNOTT A.P.E.	c Walters	b Walker	8	6–286
RANDALL D.W.	c McCosker	b Thomson	0	8–286
OLD C.M.	c Walters	b Walker	0	7–286
LEVER J.K.	c Marsh	b Thomson	3	9–305
UNDERWOOD D.L.	not	out	12	
WILLIS R.G.D.	c Marsh	b Thomson	0	10–305
EXTRAS (B – 5, LB – 9, NB – 2, W – 1)			17	
		TOTAL	305	

Bowling

	OVERS	MDNS.	RUNS	WKTS.
Thomson	24·4	3	86	4
Pascoe	26	2	96	3
Walker	35	13	56	2
Chappell	12	2	24	0
O'Keeffe	15	7	26	1

Australia – 2nd Innings

				FALL OF WICKETS
ROBINSON R.D.	c Woolmer	b Old	4	1–5
MCCOSKER R.B.		b Willis	1	2–5
CHAPPELL G.S.	c Lever	b Old	24	3–48
HOOKES D.W.	c and	b Willis	50	6–102
WALTERS K.D.	c sub. (Ealham)	b Underwood	10	4–64
SERJEANT C.S.	c Amiss	b Underwood	3	5–71
MARSH R.W.	not	out	6	
O'KEEFFE K.J.	not	out	8	
EXTRAS (NB – 8)			8	
TOTAL (six wickets)			114	

Bowling

	OVERS	MDNS.	RUNS	WKTS.
Willis	10	1	40	2
Old	14	0	46	2
Underwood	10	3	16	2
Lever	5	2	4	0

RESULT – MATCH DRAWN

Second Test
Old Trafford

FIRST DAY (Thursday 7 July)

Australia – 1st Innings

				FALL OF WICKETS
MCCOSKER R.B.	c Old	b Willis	2	1–4
DAVIS I.C.	c Knott	b Old	34	3–96
CHAPPELL G.S.	c Knott	b Greig	44	2–80
SERJEANT C.S.	l.b.w.	b Lever	14	4–125
WALTERS K.D.	c Greig	b Miller	88	7–246
HOOKES D.W.	c Knott	b Lever	5	5–140
MARSH R.W.	c Amiss	b Miller	36	6–238
BRIGHT R.J.	not	out	1	
O'KEEFFE K.J.	not	out	0	
EXTRAS (LB – 14, NB – 9)			23	
TOTAL (seven wickets)			247	

Bowling

	OVERS	MDNS.	RUNS	WKTS.
Willis	14	6	37	1
Lever	19	7	32	2
Old	20	3	57	1
Underwood	16	6	47	0
Greig	13	4	37	1
Miller	6	1	14	2

SECOND DAY (Friday 8 July)

Australia – 1st Innings

				FALL OF WICKETS
MCCOSKER R.B.	c Old	b Willis	2	1–4
DAVIS I.C.	c Knott	b Old	34	3–96
CHAPPELL G.S.	c Knott	b Greig	44	2–80
SERJEANT C.J.	l.b.w.	b Lever	14	4–125
WALTERS K.D.	c Greig	b Miller	88	7–246
HOOKES D.W.	c Knott	b Lever	5	5–140
MARSH R.W.	c Amiss	b Miller	36	6–238
BRIGHT R.J.	c Greig	b Lever	12	9–272
O'KEEFFE K.J.	c Knott	b Willis	12	8–272
WALKER M.H.N.		b Underwood	9	10–297
THOMSON J.R.	not	out	14	
EXTRAS (LB – 15, NB – 12)			27	
		TOTAL	297	

Bowling

	OVERS	MDNS.	RUNS	WKTS.
Willis	21	8	45	2
Lever	25	8	60	3
Old	20	3	57	1
Underwood	20·2	7	53	1
Greig	13	4	37	1
Miller	10	3	18	2

England – 1st Innings

				FALL OF WICKETS
AMISS D.L.	c Chappell	b Walker	11	2–23
BREARLEY J.M.	c Chappell	b Thomson	6	1–19
WOOLMER R.A.	not	out	82	
RANDALL D.W.	l.b.w.	b Bright	79	3–165
GREIG A.W.	not	out	16	
EXTRAS (B – 2, LB – 6, NB – 4)			12	
	TOTAL (three wickets)		206	

Bowling

	OVERS	MDNS.	RUNS	WKTS.
Thomson	18	4	39	1
Walker	25	6	68	1
Bright	18	4	43	1
O'Keeffe	10	2	44	0

It looks as though Derek Randall has 'worked' this ball from O'Keeffe from outside the off stump to mid-on or mid-wicket. He developed the habit of moving too far across towards the off side and frequently getting l.b.w.

THIRD DAY (Saturday 9 July)

Australia – First Innings 297

England – 1st Innings

				FALL OF WICKETS
AMISS D.L.	c Chappell	b Walker	11	2–23
BREARLEY J.M.	c Chappell	b Thomson	6	1–19
WOOLMER R.A.	c Davis	b O'Keeffe	137	4–325
RANDALL D.W.	l.b.w.	b Bright	79	3–165
GREIG A.W.	c and	b Walker	76	5–348
KNOTT A.P.E.	c O'Keeffe	b Thomson	39	7–377
MILLER G.	c Marsh	b Thomson	6	6–366
OLD C.M.	c Marsh	b Walker	37	9–435
LEVER J.K.		b Bright	10	8–404
UNDERWOOD D.L.	not	out	10	
WILLIS R.G.D.	not	out	1	
EXTRAS (B – 8, LB – 9, NB – 7)			24	
TOTAL (nine wickets)			436	

Bowling

	OVERS	MDNS.	RUNS	WKTS.
Thomson	37	10	73	3
Walker	54	15	131	3
Bright	35	11	69	2
O'Keeffe	36	11	114	1
Chappell	6	1	25	0

FOURTH DAY (Monday 11 July)

Australia – First Innings 297

England – 1st Innings

				FALL OF WICKETS
AMISS D.L.	c Chappell	b Walker	11	2–23
BREARLEY J.M.	c Chappell	b Thomson	6	1–19
WOOLMER R.A.	c Davis	b O'Keeffe	137	4–325
RANDALL D.W.	l.b.w.	b Bright	79	3–165
GREIG A.W.	c and	b Walker	76	5–348
KNOTT A.P.E.	c O'Keeffe	b Thomson	39	7–377
MILLER G.	c Marsh	b Thomson	6	6–366
OLD C.M.	c Marsh	b Walker	37	9–435
LEVER J.K.		b Bright	10	8–404
UNDERWOOD D.L.		b Bright	10	10–437
WILLIS R.G.D.	not	out	1	
EXTRAS (B – 9, LB – 9, NB – 7)			25	
		TOTAL	437	

Bowling

	OVERS	MDNS.	RUNS	WKTS.
Thomson	38	11	73	3
Walker	54	15	131	3
Bright	35·1	12	69	3
O'Keeffe	36	11	114	1
Chappell	6	1	25	0

Australia – 2nd Innings

				FALL OF WICKETS
MCCOSKER R.B.	c Underwood	b Willis	0	1–0
DAVIS I.C.	c Lever	b Willis	12	2–30
CHAPPELL G.S.		b Underwood	112	8–202
SERJEANT C.S.	c Woolmer	b Underwood	8	3–74
WALTERS K.D.	l.b.w.	b Greig	10	4–92
HOOKES D.W.	c Brearley	b Miller	28	5–146
MARSH R.W.	c Randall	b Underwood	1	6–147
BRIGHT R.J.	c and	b Underwood	0	7–147
O'KEEFFE K.J.	not	out	24	
WALKER M.H.N.	c Greig	b Underwood	6	9–212
THOMSON J.R.	c Randall	b Underwood	1	10–218
EXTRAS (LB – 1, NB – 14, W – 1)			16	
		TOTAL	218	

Bowling

	OVERS	MDNS.	RUNS	WKTS.
Willis	16	2	56	2
Lever	4	1	11	0
Underwood	32·5	13	66	6
Old	8	1	26	0
Greig	12	6	19	1
Miller	9	2	24	1

England – 2nd Innings

AMISS D.L.	not	out	0
BREARLEY J.M.	not	out	6
EXTRAS (LB – 1, NB – 1)			2
			8

Bowling

	OVERS	MDNS.	RUNS	WKTS.
Thomson	2	1	4	0
Walker	1	0	2	0

The view second slip would have of Derek Underwood about to bowl

FIFTH DAY (Tuesday 12 July)

Australia – First Innings 297

Australia – Second Innings 218

England – First Innings 437

England – 2nd Innings

				FALL OF WICKETS
AMISS D.L.	not	out	28	
BREARLEY J.M.	c Walters	b O'Keeffe	44	1–75
WOOLMER R.A.	not	out	0	
EXTRAS (LB – 3, NB – 7)			10	
TOTAL (one wicket)			82	

Bowling

	OVERS	MDNS.	RUNS	WKTS.
Thomson	8	2	24	0
Walker	7	0	17	0
O'Keeffe	9·1	4	25	1
Bright	5	2	6	0

RESULT – ENGLAND WON BY 9 WICKETS

Third Test
Trent Bridge

FIRST DAY (Thursday 28 July)

Australia – 1st Innings

				FALL OF WICKETS
MCCOSKER R.B.	c Brearley	b Hendrick	51	2–101
DAVIS I.C.	c Botham	b Underwood	33	1–79
CHAPPELL G.S.		b Botham	19	3–131
HOOKES D.W.	c Hendrick	b Willis	17	4–133
WALTERS K.D.	c Hendrick	b Botham	11	5–153
ROBINSON R.D.	c Brearley	b Greig	11	6–153
MARSH R.W.	l.b.w.	b Botham	0	7–153
O'KEEFFE K.J.	not	out	48	
WALKER M.H.N.	c Hendrick	b Botham	0	8–155
THOMSON J.R.	c Knott	b Botham	21	9–196
PASCOE L.S.	c Greig	b Hendrick	20	10–243
EXTRAS (B – 4, LB – 2, NB – 6)			12	
TOTAL			243	

Bowling

	OVERS	MDNS.	RUNS	WKTS.
Willis	15	0	58	1
Hendrick	21·2	6	46	2
Botham	20	5	74	5
Greig	15	4	35	1
Underwood	11	5	18	1

England – 1st Innings

BREARLEY J.M.	not	out	5
BOYCOTT G.	not	out	1
EXTRAS (NB – 3)			3
TOTAL (no wicket)			9

Bowling

	OVERS	MDNS.	RUNS	WKTS.
Thomson	2	1	2	0
Pascoe	1	0	4	0

SECOND DAY (Friday 29 July)

Australia – First Innings 243

England – 1st Innings

				FALL OF WICKETS
BREARLEY J.M.	c Hookes	b Pascoe	15	1–34
BOYCOTT G.	not	out	88	
WOOLMER R.A.	l.b.w.	b Pascoe	0	2–34
RANDALL D.W.	run	out	13	3–52
GREIG A.W.		b Thomson	11	4–64
MILLER G.	c Robinson	b Pascoe	13	5–82
KNOTT A.P.E.	not	out	87	
EXTRAS (B – 1, LB – 3, NB – 11)			15	
TOTAL (five wickets)			242	

Bowling

	OVERS	MDNS.	RUNS	WKTS.
Thomson	18	5	51	1
Pascoe	21	5	54	3
Walker	24	6	55	0
Chappell	8	0	19	0
O'Keeffe	11	4	43	0
Walters	3	0	5	0

Ian Botham in his
highly successful
debut for England. As
is usual for seam
bowlers, he holds the
ball with the seam
pointing down the
pitch between
forefinger and second
finger. The umpire is
David Constant

THIRD DAY (Saturday 30 July)

Australia – First Innings 243

England – 1st Innings

				FALL OF WICKETS
BREARLEY J.M.	c Hookes	b Pascoe	15	1–34
BOYCOTT G.	c McCosker	b Thomson	107	6–297
WOOLMER R.A.	l.b.w.	b Pascoe	0	2–34
RANDALL D.W.	run	out	13	3–52
GREIG A.W.		b Thomson	11	4–64
MILLER G.	c Robinson	b Pascoe	13	5–82
KNOTT A.P.E.	c Davis	b Thomson	135	7–326
BOTHAM I.T.		b Walker	25	9–357
UNDERWOOD D.L.		b Pascoe	7	8–357
HENDRICK M.		b Walker	1	10–364
WILLIS R.G.D.	not	out	2	
EXTRAS (B – 9, LB – 7, NB – 16, W – 3)			35	
		TOTAL	364	

Bowling

	OVERS	MDNS.	RUNS	WKTS.
Thomson	31	6	103	3
Pascoe	32	10	80	4
Walker	39·2	12	79	2
Chappell	8	0	19	0
O'Keeffe	11	4	43	0
Walters	3	0	5	0

Australia – 2nd Innings

				FALL OF WICKETS
MCCOSKER R.B.	not	out	40	
DAVIS I.C.	c Greig	b Willis	9	1–18
CHAPPELL G.S.		b Hendrick	27	2–60
HOOKES D.W.	not	out	31	
EXTRAS (NB – 5)			5	
	TOTAL (two wickets)		112	

Bowling

	OVERS	MDNS.	RUNS	WKTS.
Willis	10	2	33	1
Hendrick	11	4	28	1
Botham	13	3	33	0
Greig	3	1	5	0
Underwood	8	6	8	0

Third Test, third day:
Hookes

FOURTH DAY (Monday 1 August)

Australia – First Innings 243

England – First Innings 364

Australia – 2nd Innings

					FALL OF WICKETS
MCCOSKER R.B.	c Brearley	b Willis	107		5–240
DAVIS I.C.	c Greig	b Willis	9		1–18
CHAPPELL G.S.		b Hendrick	27		2–60
HOOKES D.W.	l.b.w.	b Hendrick	42		3–154
WALTERS K.D.	c Randall	b Greig	28		4–204
ROBINSON R.D.	l.b.w.	b Underwood	34		7–270
MARSH R.W.	c Greig	b Willis	0		6–240
O'KEEFFE K.J.	not	out	21		
WALKER M.H.N.		b Willis	17		8–307
THOMSON J.R.		b Willis	0		9–308
PASCOE L.S.	c Hendrick	b Underwood	0		10–309
EXTRAS (B – 1, LB – 5, NB – 17, W – 1)			24		
		TOTAL	309		

Bowling

	OVERS	MDNS.	RUNS	WKTS.
Willis	26	6	88	5
Hendrick	32	14	56	2
Botham	25	5	60	0
Greig	9	2	24	1
Underwood	27	15	49	2
Miller	5	2	5	0
Woolmer	3	0	3	0

England – 2nd Innings

BREARLEY J.M.	not	out	5
BOYCOTT G.	not	out	12
	TOTAL (no wicket)		17

Bowling

	OVERS	MDNS.	RUNS	WKTS.
Thomson	4	1	10	0
Pascoe	3	1	7	0

FIFTH DAY (Tuesday 2 August)

Australia – First Innings 243

Australia – Second Innings 309

England – First Innings 364

England – 2nd Innings

				FALL OF WICKETS
BREARLEY J.M.		b Walker	81	1–154
BOYCOTT G.	not	out	80	
KNOTT A.P.E.	c O'Keeffe	b Walker	2	2–156
GREIG A.W.		b Walker	0	3–158
RANDALL D.W.	not	out	19	
EXTRAS (B – 2, LB – 2, NB – 2, W – 1)			7	
TOTAL (three wickets)			189	

Bowling

	OVERS	MDNS.	RUNS	WKTS.
Thomson	16	6	34	0
Pascoe	22	6	43	0
O'Keeffe	19·2	2	65	0
Walker	24	8	40	3

RESULT – ENGLAND WON BY 7 WICKETS

Left: Third Test, fourth day: Thomson b. Willis 0

Fourth Test
Headingley

FIRST DAY (Thursday 11 August)

England – 1st Innings

				FALL OF WICKETS
BREARLEY J.M.	c Marsh	b Thomson	0	1–0
BOYCOTT G.	not	out	110	
WOOLMER R.A.	c Chappell	b Thomson	37	2–82
RANDALL D.W.	l.b.w.	b Pascoe	20	3–105
GREIG A.W.		b Thomson	43	4–201
ROOPE G.R.J.	not	out	19	
EXTRAS (B – 1, LB – 3, NB – 17, W – 2)			23	
TOTAL (four wickets)			252	

Bowling

	OVERS	MDNS.	RUNS	WKTS.
Thomson	21	4	78	3
Walker	27	12	59	0
Pascoe	20	7	48	1
Walters	3	0	5	0
Bright	6	3	14	0
Chappell	10	2	25	0

Right: Fourth Test, first day: Boycott hooks Thomson on the way to his hundredth first-class 100

SECOND DAY (Friday 12 August)

England – 1st Innings

				FALL OF WICKETS
BREARLEY J.M.	c Marsh	b Thomson	0	1–0
BOYCOTT G.	c Chappell	b Pascoe	191	10–436
WOOLMER R.A.	c Chappell	b Thomson	37	2–82
RANDALL D.W.	l.b.w.	b Pascoe	20	3–105
GREIG A.W.		b Thomson	43	4–201
ROOPE G.R.J.	c Walters	b Thomson	34	5–275
KNOTT A.P.E.	l.b.w.	b Bright	57	6–398
BOTHAM I.T.		b Bright	0	7–398
UNDERWOOD D.L.	c Bright	b Pascoe	6	8–412
HENDRICK M.	c Robinson	b Pascoe	4	9–422
WILLIS R.G.D.	not	out	5	
EXTRAS (B – 5, LB – 9, NB – 22, W – 3)			39	
TOTAL			436	

Bowling

	OVERS	MDNS.	RUNS	WKTS.
Thomson	34	7	113	4
Walker	48	21	97	0
Pascoe	34·4	10	91	4
Walters	3	1	5	0
Bright	26	9	66	2
Chappell	10	2	25	0

Australia – 1st Innings

				FALL OF WICKETS
MCCOSKER R.B.	run	out	27	3–52
DAVIS I.C.	l.b.w.	b Hendrick	0	1–8
CHAPPELL G.S.	c Brearley	b Hendrick	4	2–26
HOOKES D.W.	l.b.w.	b Botham	24	4–57
WALTERS K.D.	c Hendrick	b Botham	4	5–66

ROBINSON R.D.	not	out	6
MARSH R.W.	not	out	0
EXTRAS (NB − 2)			2
		TOTAL (five wickets)	67

Bowling

	OVERS	MDNS.	RUNS	WKTS.
Willis	5	0	35	0
Hendrick	10	2	21	2
Botham	5	1	9	2

THIRD DAY (Saturday 13 August)

England – First Innings 436

Australia – 1st Innings

				FALL OF WICKETS
MCCOSKER R.B.	run	out	27	3–52
DAVIS I.C.	l.b.w.	b Hendrick	0	1–8
CHAPPELL G.S.	c Brearley	b Hendrick	4	2–26
HOOKES D.W.	l.b.w.	b Botham	24	4–57
WALTERS K.D.	c Hendrick	b Botham	4	5–66
ROBINSON R.D.	c Greig	b Hendrick	20	7–87
MARSH R.W.	c Knott	b Botham	2	6–77
BRIGHT R.J.	not	out	9	
WALKER M.H.N.	c Knott	b Botham	7	8–100
THOMSON J.R.		b Botham	0	9–100
PASCOE L.S.		b Hendrick	0	10–103
EXTRAS (LB − 3, NB − 2, W − 1)			6	
		TOTAL	103	

Bowling

	OVERS	MDNS.	RUNS	WKTS.
Willis	5	0	35	0
Hendrick	15·3	2	41	4
Botham	11	3	21	5

Australia – 2nd Innings

					FALL OF WICKETS
MCCOSKER R.B.	c Knott	b Greig		12	2–35
DAVIS I.C.	c Knott	b Greig		19	1–31
CHAPPELL G.S.	not	out		29	
HOOKES D.W.	l.b.w.	b Hendrick		21	3–63
WALTERS K.D.	l.b.w.	b Woolmer		15	4–97
ROBINSON R.D.	not	out		11	
EXTRAS (LB – 2, NB – 9, W – 2)				13	
TOTAL (four wickets)				120	

Bowling

	OVERS	MDNS.	RUNS	WKTS.
Willis	6·2	3	9	0
Hendrick	11	2	29	1
Greig	16	7	43	2
Botham	11	3	19	0
Woolmer	5	3	5	1
Underwood	3	2	2	0

FOURTH DAY (Monday 15 August)

England – First Innings 436

Australia – First Innings 103

Australia – 2nd Innings

				FALL OF WICKETS
MCCOSKER R.B.	c Knott	b Greig	12	2–35
DAVIS I.C.	c Knott	b Greig	19	1–31
CHAPPELL G.S.	c Greig	b Willis	36	5–130
HOOKES D.W.	l.b.w.	b Hendrick	21	3–63
WALTERS K.D.	l.b.w.	b Woolmer	15	4–97
ROBINSON R.D.		b Hendrick	20	6–167
MARSH R.W.	c Randall	b Hendrick	63	10–248
BRIGHT R.J.	c Greig	b Hendrick	5	7–179
WALKER M.H.N.		b Willis	30	8–244
THOMSON J.R.		b Willis	0	9–245
PASCOE L.S.	not	out	0	
EXTRAS (B – 1, LB – 4, NB – 18, W – 4)			27	
		TOTAL	248	

Bowling

	OVERS	MDNS.	RUNS	WKTS.
Willis	14	7	32	3
Hendrick	22·5	6	54	4
Greig	20	7	64	2
Botham	17	3	47	0
Woolmer	8	4	8	1
Underwood	8	3	16	0

RESULT – ENGLAND WON BY AN INNINGS AND 85 RUNS

Fifth Test
The Oval

FIRST DAY (Thursday 25 August)

RAIN. NO PLAY.

SECOND DAY (Friday 26 August)

England – 1st Innings

				FALL OF WICKETS
BREARLEY J.M.	c Marsh	b Malone	39	2–88
BOYCOTT G.	c McCosker	b Walker	39	1–86
WOOLMER R.A.	l.b.w.	b Thomson	15	4–104
RANDALL D.W.	c Marsh	b Malone	3	3–104
GREIG A.W.	c Bright	b Malone	0	5–106
ROOPE G.R.J.		b Thomson	38	8–169
KNOTT A.P.E.	c McCosker	b Malone	6	6–122
LEVER J.K.	l.b.w.	b Malone	3	7–130
UNDERWOOD D.L.		b Thomson	20	9–174
HENDRICK M.	not	out	1	
WILLIS R.G.D.	not	out	6	
EXTRAS (LB – 5, NB – 5, W – 1)			11	
TOTAL (nine wickets)			181	

Bowling

	OVERS	MDNS.	RUNS	WKTS.
Thomson	19	3	65	3
Malone	43	20	53	5
Walker	27	10	51	1
Bright	2	1	1	0

Left: Mike Hendrick looks as though he's enjoying his job. It's not surprising that fast bowlers in general, and he in particular, have problems with hamstrings and thigh muscles. Excellent follow-through. Umpire, Lloyd Budd

THIRD DAY (Saturday 27 August)

England – 1st Innings

				FALL OF WICKETS
BREARLEY J.M.	c Marsh	b Malone	39	2–88
BOYCOTT G.	c McCosker	b Walker	39	1–86
WOOLMER R.A.	l.b.w.	b Thomson	15	4–104
RANDALL D.W.	c Marsh	b Malone	3	3–104
GREIG A.W.	c Bright	b Malone	0	5–106
ROOPE G.R.J.		b Thomson	38	8–169
KNOTT A.P.E.	c McCosker	b Malone	6	6–122
LEVER J.K.	l.b.w.	b Malone	3	7–130
UNDERWOOD D.L.		b Thomson	20	9–174
HENDRICK M.		b Thomson	15	10–214
WILLIS R.G.D.	not	out	24	
EXTRAS (LB – 6, NB – 5, W – 1)			12	
		TOTAL	214	

Bowling

	OVERS	MDNS.	RUNS	WKTS.
Thomson	23·2	3	87	4
Malone	47	20	63	5
Walker	28	11	51	1
Bright	3	2	1	0

Australia – 1st Innings

				FALL OF WICKETS
SERJEANT C.S.	l.b.w.	b Willis	0	1–0
MCCOSKER R.B.	not	out	2	
CHAPPELL G.S.	not	out	7	
EXTRAS (NB – 2)			2	
		TOTAL (one wicket)	11	

Left: Fifth Test, second day: Woolmer, l.b.w. Thomson

Bowling

	OVERS	MDNS.	RUNS	WKTS.
Willis	4	2	6	1
Hendrick	3	1	3	0

FOURTH DAY (Monday 29 August)

England – First Innings 214

Australia – 1st Innings

					FALL OF WICKETS
SERJEANT C.S.	l.b.w.	b Willis		0	1–0
MCCOSKER R.B.	l.b.w.	b Willis		32	4–84
CHAPPELL G.S.	c and	b Underwood		39	2–54
HUGHES K.J.	c Willis	b Hendrick		1	3–67
HOOKES D.W.	c Knott	b Greig		85	6–184
WALTERS K.D.		b Willis		4	5–104
MARSH R.W.	not	out		53	
BRIGHT R.J.	not	out		6	
EXTRAS (LB – 4, NB – 2)				6	
TOTAL (six wickets)				226	

Bowling

	OVERS	MDNS.	RUNS	WKTS.
Willis	19	5	55	3
Hendrick	25	5	49	1
Lever	15	4	30	0
Underwood	29	8	77	1
Greig	6	2	9	1

Max Walker

FIFTH DAY (Tuesday 30 August)

England – First Innings 214

Australia – 1st Innings

				FALL OF WICKETS
SERJEANT C.S.	l.b.w.	b Willis	0	1–0
MCCOSKER R.B.	l.b.w.	b Willis	32	4–84
CHAPPELL G.S.	c and	b Underwood	39	2–54
HUGHES K.J.	c Willis	b Hendrick	1	3–67
HOOKES D.W.	c Knott	b Greig	85	6–184
WALTERS K.D.		b Willis	4	5–104
MARSH R.W.	l.b.w.	b Hendrick	57	7–236
BRIGHT R.J.	l.b.w.	b Willis	16	8–252
WALKER M.H.N.	not	out	78	
MALONE M.F.		b Lever	46	9–352
THOMSON J.R.		b Willis	17	10–385
EXTRAS (B – 1, LB – 6, NB – 3)			10	
		TOTAL	385	

Bowling

	OVERS	MDNS.	RUNS	WKTS.
Willis	29·3	5	102	5
Hendrick	37	5	93	2
Lever	22	6	61	1
Underwood	35	9	102	1
Greig	8	2	17	1

England – 2nd Innings

				FALL OF WICKETS
BREARLEY J.M.	c Serjeant	b Thomson	4	1–5
BOYCOTT G.	not	out	25	
WOOLMER R.A.	c Marsh	b Malone	6	2–16
RANDALL D.W.	not	out	20	
EXTRAS (W – 2)			2	
		TOTAL (two wickets)	57	

Bowling

	OVERS	MDNS.	RUNS	WKTS.
Thomson	5	1	22	1
Malone	10	4	14	1
Walker	8	2	14	0
Bright	3	2	5	0

RESULT – MATCH DRAWN

Fifth Test, last day

1977

Final Test Match Averages

England

NAME	M.	I.	N.O.	RUNS	H.S.	AVER.	100	50	OVERS	MDNS.	RUNS	WKTS.	AVER.	CT.	ST.
AMISS D.L.	2	4	1	43	28*	14·33	—	—	—	—	—	—	—	2	—
BARLOW G.D.	1	2	0	6	5	3·00	—	—	—	—	—	—	—	—	—
BOTHAM I.T.	2	2	0	25	25	12·50	—	—	73	16	202	10	20·20	1	—
BOYCOTT G.	3	5	2	442	191	147·33	2	1	—	—	—	—	—	—	—
BREARLEY J.M.	5	9	0	247	81	27·44	—	1	—	—	—	—	—	7	—
GREIG A.W.	5	7	0	226	91	32·28	—	2	77	25	196	7	28·00	9	—
HENDRICK M.	3	3	0	20	15	6·66	—	—	128·4	33	290	14	20·71	5	—
KNOTT A.P.E.	5	7	0	255	135	36·42	1	1	—	—	—	—	—	12	—
LEVER J.K.	3	4	0	24	10	6·00	—	—	75	22	197	5	39·40	2	—
MILLER G.	2	2	0	19	13	9·50	—	—	24	7	47	3	15·66	—	—
OLD C.M.	2	3	0	46	37	15·33	—	—	77	14	199	5	39·80	2	—
RANDALL D.W.	5	8	2	207	79	34·50	—	2	—	—	—	—	—	4	—
ROOPE G.R.J.	2	2	0	72	38	36·00	—	—	—	—	—	—	—	—	—
UNDERWOOD D.L.	5	6	2	66	20	16·50	—	—	169·1	61	362	13	27·83	3	—
WILLIS R.G.D.	5	6	4	49	24*	24·50	—	—	166·4	36	534	27	19·77	2	—
WOOLMER R.A.	5	8	1	394	137	56·28	2	1	16	5	31	1	31·00	2	—
												CT. SUB.	2	—

extras 159   run out 1

TOTAL RUNS SCORED	2300	TOTAL WICKETS TAKEN	86
WICKETS LOST	66		
AVERAGE RUNS PER WICKET	34·48		

Australia

NAME	M.	I.	N.O.	RUNS	H.S.	AVER.	100	50	OVERS	MDNS.	RUNS	WKTS.	AVER.	CT.	ST.
BRIGHT R.J.	3	5	1	42	16	10·50	—	—	72·1	27	147	5	29·40	2	—
CHAPPELL G.S.	5	9	0	371	112	41·22	1	1	39	5	105	0	∝	6	—
DAVIS I.C.	3	6	0	107	34	17·83	—	—	—	—	—	—	—	2	—
HOOKES D.W.	5	9	0	283	85	31·44	—	2	—	—	—	—	—	1	—
HUGHES K.J.	1	1	0	1	1	1·00	—	—	—	—	—	—	—	—	—
MALONE M.F.	1	1	0	46	46	46·00	—	—	57	24	77	6	12·83	—	—
MARSH R.W.	5	9	1	166	63	20·75	—	2	—	—	—	—	—	9	—
MCCOSKER R.B.	5	9	0	255	107	28·33	1	1	—	—	—	—	—	5	—
O'KEEFFE K.J.	3	6	4	125	48*	62·50	—	—	100·3	31	305	3	101·66	3	—
PASCOE L.S.	3	5	2	23	20	7·66	—	—	137·4	35	363	13	27·92	—	—
ROBINSON R.D.	3	6	0	100	34	16·66	—	—	—	—	—	—	—	4	—
SERJEANT C.S.	3	5	0	106	81	21·20	—	1	—	—	—	—	—	1	—
THOMSON J.R.	5	8	1	59	21	8·42	—	—	200·5	44	583	23	25·34	—	—
WALKER M.H.N.	5	8	1	151	78*	21·57	—	1	273·2	88	551	14	39·35	1	—
WALTERS K.D.	5	9	0	223	88	24·77	—	2	6	1	10	0	∝	5	—
												CT. SUB.	—	—

extras   155   run out   2

TOTAL RUNS SCORED   2213   TOTAL WICKETS TAKEN   66

WICKETS LOST   86

AVERAGE RUNS PER WICKET   25·73

1977

First Class Averages of English Test Team

Batting

NAME	I.	N.O.	RUNS	H.S.	AVER.	100	POSITION IN ENGLISH AVERAGES
AMISS D.L.	34	5	1513	162*	52·17	6	7
BARLOW G.D.	34	4	658	80	21·93	–	128
BOTHAM I.T.	27	3	738	114	30·75	1	57
BOYCOTT G.	30	5	1701	191	68·04	7	2
BREARLEY J.M.	31	4	1251	152	46·33	3	14
GREIG A.W.	24	0	735	88	30·62	–	60
HENDRICK M.	16	6	66	17	6·60	–	unplaced
KNOTT A.P.E.	20	2	771	135	42·83	2	21
LEVER J.K.	17	4	73	11	5·61	–	unplaced
MILLER G.	30	3	730	86*	27·03	–	85
OLD C.M.	13	2	341	107	31·00	1	55
RANDALL D.W.	33	3	709	79	23·63	–	115
ROOPE G.R.J.	31	5	1431	115	55·03	5	5
UNDERWOOD D.L.	19	6	91	20	7·00	–	unplaced
WILLIS R.G.D.	15	5	124	29	12·40	–	205
WOOLMER R.A.	30	4	1238	137	47·61	6	11

Bowling

NAME	OVERS	MDNS.	RUNS	WKTS.	AVER.	POSITION IN ENGLISH AVERAGES
AMISS D.L.	—	—	—	—	—	—
BARLOW G.D.	—	—	—	—	—	—
BOTHAM I.T.	665·5	149	1983	88	22·53	32
BOYCOTT G.	10	4	16	1	16·00	unplaced
BREARLEY J.M.	—	—	—	—	—	—
GREIG A.W.	313·2	90	850	35	24·28	45
HENDRICK M.	562·3	189	1068	67	15·94	2
KNOTT A.P.E.	—	—	—	—	—	—
LEVER J.K.	504·4	123	1303	58	22·46	31
MILLER G.	655·4	224	1551	87	17·82	6
OLD C.M.	280·4	69	680	30	22·66	33
RANDALL D.W.	1	0	1	0	∞	unplaced
ROOPE G.R.J.	51·3	7	155	3	51·66	unplaced
UNDERWOOD D.L.	436·2	164	896	46	19·47	9
WILLIS R.G.D.	399	94	1183	58	20·39	17
WOOLMER R.A.	134·1	50	289	19	15·21	1

Test Career Averages (to 30 September 1977)

ENGLAND

	M.	I.	N.O.	RUNS	H.S.	AVER.	100	50	BALLS	RUNS	WKTS.	AVER.	CT.	ST.
AMISS D.L.	50	88	10	3612	262*	46·30	11	11					24	
BARLOW G.D.	3	5	1	17	7*	4·25								
BOTHAM I.T.	2	2	0	25	25	12·50			438	202	10	20·20	1	
BOYCOTT G.	66	115	16	5021	246*	50·71	14	27	792	346	7	49·42	20	1
BREARLEY J.M.	13	23	0	587	91	25·52		3					18	
GREIG A.W.	58	93	4	3599	148	40·43	8	20	9802	4541	141	32·20	87	
HENDRICK M.	13	13	5	45	15	5·62			2542	1100	42	26·19	16	
KNOTT A.P.E.	89	138	14	4175	135	33·66	5	28					233	19
LEVER J.K.	9	14	1	161	53	12·38		1	1612	708	35	20·22	7	
MILLER G.	3	4	0	79	36	19·75			306	153	4	38·25		
OLD C.M.	33	49	6	671	65	15·60		2	6024	3032	102	29·72	21	
RANDALL D.W.	10	17	2	471	174	31·40	1	2					7	
ROOPE G.R.J.	11	18	1	451	77	26·52		3	156	72	0	∝	18	
UNDERWOOD D.L.	74	100	31	824	45*	11·94			18979	6600	265	24·90	39	
WILLIS R.G.D.	29	45	24	257	24*	12·23			5457	2746	105	26·15	17	
WOOLMER R.A.	15	26	1	920	149	36·80	3	2	546	299	4	74·75	8	

AUSTRALIA

	M.	I.	N.O.	RUNS	H.S.	AVER.	100	50	BALLS	RUNS	WKTS.	AVER.	CT.	ST.
BRIGHT R.J.	3	5	1	42	16	10·50			433	147	5	29·40	2	
CHAPPELL G.S.	51	90	13	4097	247*	53·20	14	20	3752	1399	32	43·71	73	
DAVIS I.C.	15	27	1	692	105	26·61	1	4					9	
HOOKES D.W.	6	11	0	356	85	32·36		3					2	
HUGHES K.J.	1	1	0	1	1	1·00								
MALONE M.F.	1	1	0	46	46	46·00			342	77	6	12·83		
MARSH R.W.	52	82	9	2396	132	32·82	3	12					190	8
MCCOSKER R.B.	22	40	5	1498	127	42·80	4	9					18	
O'KEEFFE K.J.	24	34	9	644	85	25·76		1	5384	2018	53	38·07	15	
PASCOE L.S.	3	5	2	23	20	7·66			826	363	13	27·92		
ROBINSON R.D.	3	6	0	100	34	16·66							4	
SERJEANT C.S.	3	5	0	106	81	21·20		1					1	
THOMSON J.R.	22	25	4	288	49	13·71			5083	2607	103	25·31	9	
WALKER M.H.N.	34	43	13	586	78*	19·53		1	10094	3792	138	27·47	12	
WALTERS K.D.	68	116	12	4960	250	47·69	14	30	3211	1378	49	28·12	38	

Index

References to illustration captions are in italic; roman figures refer to the colour plates between pages 16 and 17 and 80 and 81